JOHN F. KENNEDY

The biography of JFK, the man behind the
assassination. The history of the USA president
who lead the white house

Chapter one

The man John f. Kennedy

John fitzgerald Kennedy (may 29, 1917 -- November 22, 1963), frequently known from the initials JFK and jack, has been an American boxer who functioned since the 35th president of the USA in january 1961 until his assassination in November 1963. Kennedy functioned in the peak of their cold war, and also the vast majority of his job as president worried connections together with the soviet union and Cuba. Even a democrat," Kennedy represented Massachusetts at the U.S. House of reps and senate before getting president.

Kennedy was born in to a rich political family at brookline, Massachusetts. He graduated from harvard university in 1940, previous to linking the U.S. Naval reserve the next calendar year. Throughout world war ii he controlled a streak of pt boats in the pacific theatre and also got the navy and marine corps medal because of his services. Subsequent to the war, the Kennedy represented the Massachusetts's 11th congressional district at the U.S. House of representatives from 1947 to 1953. He was then chosen for the U.S. Senate and functioned while the junior senator from Massachusetts by 1953 to 1960. While from the senate," Kennedy released his novel profiles in courage, which won a pulitzer prize. From the 1960 presidential elections he defeated republican rival richard nixon, that was simply the vice president.

Kennedy's administration comprised high pressures with nordic nations from the cold war. Like a consequence, he raised the amount of American military advisors in south Vietnam. Back in april 1961 he approved an effort to overthrow the Cuban government of fidel castro at the bay of pigs invasion. Kennedy licensed the Cuban challenge at November 1961. He chased operation northwoods (intends for fictitious flag strikes to put on acceptance for a war against

Cuba) at march 1962. But his government continued to fund an invasion of Cuba at the summer months of 1962. The subsequent oct, U.S. Spy planes discovered soviet missile bases were set up in Cuba; yet the consequent span of anxieties, known as the Cuban missile crisis, not quite caused the break out of the international thermo nuclear battle. The strategic hamlet plan started in viet nam throughout his presidency. Domestically," Kennedy presided on the constitution of this peace corps along with also the continuation of this apollo space application. In addition, he affirmed that the civil rights movements, but has been merely marginally effective in passing his new frontier national coverages.

But on November 22, 1963, he had been imprisoned in Dallas, Texas. Vice president lyndon b. Johnson assumed the presidency up on Kennedy's departure. Former and prior U.S. Maritime lee harvey Oswald was detained for its nation offense, but he had been captured and murdered by jack ruby two weeks after. Even the FBI and the warren commission both equally reasoned Oswald had acted alone in the assassination, however many classes contested the warren report and felt Kennedy had been the casualty of the conspiracy. Right after Kennedy's departure, congress enacted several of the suggestions, such as the civil rights act and also the income act of 1964. Kennedy rankings tremendously in surveys of U.S. Presidents with historians and also the overall populace. His private existence has already been the target of substantial continued attention, after general public revelations at the 1970 s of the continual health disorders and extra marital affairs.

Early-life and education

John fitzgerald Kennedy was created may 29, 1917, in 83 beal's street at the boston suburb of brookline, Massachusetts, to joseph p. Kennedy sr., also a businessman and fighter, also rose Kennedy (née fitz-gerald), also a philanthropist and socialite. His paternal grandfather, p. J. Kennedy, was a Massachusetts state senator. Kennedy's maternal grandfather and namesake, John f. Fitzgerald, functioned being a U.S. Congressman and has been chosen to two terms as mayor of boston. Each of the grandparents were all children of irish immigrants. Kennedy was an older god, joseph jr., along with seven young sisters: rosemary, kathleen ("kick"), eunice, patricia, robert ("bobby"), jean, also edward ("ted").

Kennedy dwelt in brookline for its very first 10 decades of his lifetime and also attended to the regional st. Aidan's church, at which he had been baptized on june 1 9, 1917. He had been educated in the edward devotion college at brookline, both the noble and greenough decrease college at dedham, Massachusetts, and also the dexter college (additionally in brookline) throughout the

4th grade. His dad's firm had retained him from your family for very long stretches of time, along with also his ventures ended up focused on wall street and hollywood. Back in september 1927, the family transferred out of brookline into the riverdale area of nyc in june. Youthful John attended the reduce campus of riverdale country school, an exclusive college for boys, ranging from 5th to 7th grade. 2 decades after, your family proceeded into suburban bronxville, new york, at which Kennedy had been a part of boy scout troop 2. Your family summers and ancient autumns in their property in hyannis port, also a village on cape cod, Massachusetts; both xmas and easter vacations ended up in their winter season getaway at palm beach, florida. Back in september 1930," Kennedy, then 1-3 yrs of age, attended the canterbury school in new milford, connecticut, to get 8th-grade. Back in april 1931he had an appendectomy, right after he retreated from canterbury and recovered in residence.

In september 1931," Kennedy started off attending choate, a prestigious boarding school in wallingford, connecticut, for 9th through 12th grade. His elderly brother joe jr. Had been choate for a couple of decades and turned into a soccer player and resulting college student. He even spent his very first years in choate within his older brother's shadow and paid by rebellious behavior that brought a coterie. They carried their notorious stunt by bursting a bathroom chair using a powerful firecracker. From the consequent chapel meeting, the stringent headmaster," george st. John, brandished the bathroom chair and talked about specified"muckers" who'd "spit within our ocean". The rebellious Kennedy shot the cue named his own band "the muckers club", that comprised roommate and lifelong good friend kirk lemoyne" billings.

Throughout his years in choate, Kennedy was diagnosed with health issues that surfaced together with his unexpected emergency hospitalization at 1934 in yale new haven hospital, in which medical professionals imagined alcoholism. Back in june 1934he had been declared for the mayo clinic at rochester, minnesota; the greatest identification that there had been nausea. Kennedy graduated from choate at june of the next calendar year, completing 64th at a category of 112 college students. He'd become the small business manager of this college yearbook and has been voted the "likely to triumph".

Kennedy's birthplace at brookline, Massachusetts

Even the Kennedy family in hyannis port, Massachusetts, together with JFK in the high left from the snowy top, 1931

In september 1935," Kennedy left his very first excursion overseas when he flew into london together with his mother and father and his sister kathleen. He planned to examine below harold laski at the london school of economics (lse), since his elderly brother had carried out. Ill-health pushed his return into the USA at october of the calendar year, once he registered attended and late princeton college but needed to depart immediately after two weeks owing to your gastro intestinal disorder. He was hospitalized for monitoring at peter bent brigham hospital in boston. He also convalesced farther in your family home in palm beach, spent the spring of 1936 doing work like a ranch hand about the 40,000-acre jay 6 cows ranch out benson, arizona. It's documented that ranchman jack speidel functioned each brother "quite tricky".

In september 1936," Kennedy registered at harvard college, along with also his app essay said: "the grounds whom i've for needing to move to harvard are a few. Personally, i think that harvard will offer me an improved backdrop and also a far better liberal instruction than every other college. I've always needed to really go there, since i have believed it is perhaps not simply a second faculty, but is still just a university using something special to give. Afterward too i would like to visit exactly the exact same faculty because my dad. For always a 'harvard person' can be a coveted difference, and also yet one which i truly expect i will accomplish." he first produced this calendar year's yearly "freshman smoker", referred to as with means of a reviewer "an intricate amusement, that comprised within its own throw outstanding characters of this air, monitor and sports activities entire world".

He also used to its golfing, football swimming clubs and got a place on the varsity swimming club. Kennedy also drifted from the star course and won the 1936 nantucket audio star championship. Back in july 1937, Kennedy jumped to france--carrying his eponymous and spent fourteen days forcing europe together with billings. Back in june 1938," Kennedy flew overseas together along with his dad and brother to just work on the embassy in london, in which his dad was president franklin d. Roosevelt's U.S. Ambassador for the court of st. James's.

In 1939," Kennedy toured europe, the soviet union, the balkans, and also the middle east in prep because of his harvard senior honors thesis. Then moved into czechoslovakia and germany prior to returning to london on september 1, 1939, the day that germany invaded poland to indicate the onset of world war ii. Fourteen weeks after, your family has been at the home of commons for speeches constituting the united kingdom's announcement of war on germany in june. Kennedy has been delivered because his dad's consultant to aid with agreements to get western natives of their ss athenian prior to flying straight back into the U.S. Out of foynes, ireland, to port washington, new york, on his very first trans-atlantic trip.

When Kennedy had been still an upper classman in harvard that he begun to carry his scientific studies far more significantly and acquired a fascination with political doctrine. He left the dean's listing at his inaugural season old. Back in 1940 Kennedy accomplished his thesis "appeasement at munich", roughly british involvement from the munich contract. The thesis finally turned into a best seller below the title why england slept. Along with beating britain's collapse to fortify its army at the lead-up into world war ii, the publication additionally referred to as to get an anglo-American alliance contrary to the climbing infantry powers. Kennedy grew to become supportive of U.S. Intervention in world war ii, along with also his daddy's isolationist faith caused the latter's dismissal because ambassador into the uk. This produced a divide involving the Kennedy and roosevelt households.

In 1940," Kennedy graduated cum laude from harvard with a bachelor of arts in govt, focusing on global occasions. This autumn, he registered in the stanford graduate school of company and organized courses there. In ancient 1941, Kennedy helped and left his dad compose a memoir of the period within an American ambassador. Then he traveled through south America; his itinerary comprised colombia, ecuador and peru.

U.S. Navy reserve (1941--1945)

In 1940," Kennedy strove to input army's officer candidate schooling june. Irrespective of months of instruction that " he had been clinically disqualified owing to his continual back issues. On september 2 4, 1941," Kennedy, together with the assistance of subsequently manager of the office of naval intelligence (oni) and preceding naval attaché into joseph Kennedy alan kirk, combined the united states naval reserve. He had been commissioned an ensign about oct 26, 1941, also joined the team of this office of naval intelligence at washington, d.c.

Lieutenant (junior-grade) Kennedy (standing) together with his pt109 team, 1943

In january 1942," Kennedy was delegated for the oni area office in headquarters, sixth naval district, at charleston, sc. [3 3] he attended the naval reserve officer training college in north western university at chicago, illinois, from july 27 to september 27 [3 2] then voluntarily entered the motor torpedo boat squadrons coaching center at melville, rhode island. [3 3] [3-5] on october 10he had been encouraged to lieutenant junior level. [3 3] in ancient November," Kennedy was mourning the departure of his shut, youth buddy, marine corps second lieutenant george houk mead jr., who'd previously been murdered in action at guadalcanal who august and given the navy cross for his bravery. Inspired by women acquaintance out of the rich newport family, the few had ceased in middletown, rhode island in the peninsula at which the adorned, deadly secret agent, commander hugo w. Koehler, usn,'d been murdered that the prior calendar year old. Ambling round the plots close to the miniature st. Columba's chapel," Kennedy stopped in excess of koehler's white granite crossover tomb markers and pondered their or her own mortality, even trusting loud when his time arrived, he wouldn't need to perish with faith. "however, these matters cannot be faked, but" he included. "there is absolutely no bluffing." 2 years after, Kennedy along with koehler's step-son, U.S. Senator claiborne pell had turned into friends and political allies, even but they'd been occupying because the mid-1930s within their "salad days" the exact same newport debutante get together "circuit" so when pell experienced outdated kathleen ("kick") Kennedy. Kennedy accomplished his coaching about december two and has been delegated to motor torpedo squadron 4.

His first control was pt-101 in december 7, 1942, before february 2-3, 1943: it had been a patrol torpedo (pt) vessel utilized for prep while still Kennedy had been a teacher in melville. Then led about three huskins pt ships --pt-98," pt-99, along with pt-101, that were relocated from mtbron 4 at melville, rhode island back again to jacksonville, florida, and also the brand new mtbron 14 (shaped february 17, 1943). Throughout the adventure southwest, he also had been hospitalized temporarily in jacksonville soon after diving in to the coldwater into unfold a propeller. Subsequently, Kennedy had been delegated duty in panama and after from the pacific theatre, in which he finally controlled two pt ships.

Commanding pt 109

In april 1943," Kennedy was delegated to motor torpedo squadron two, also on april 2 4 he obtained control of pt109, that had been located at time tulagi island at the solomon's. At the nights august 1) --two, in service of this recent georgia effort, pt109 was on its own 31st assignment together with two different pts arranged to obstruct or repel 4 japanese destroyers and float airplanes carrying meals, provides, along with 900 japanese troops into the vila plantation garrison in the southern tip of their solomon's kolombangara island. Intelligence was shipped to Kennedy's commander thomas g. Warfield hoping the introduction of the enormous japanese naval drive which could pass to evening of august inch. Of those 2-4 torpedoes fired this night time by 8 of those American pt'snot one struck on the japanese convoy. On this dark and moonless night time, Kennedy seen a japanese destroyer heading north to its own recurrence by the bottom of kolombangara close to 2:00 a.m., also strove to reverse into strike, when pt109 was hit unexpectedly at a angle and then cut half of the destroyer amangiri, murdering two pt109 team members.

Kennedy gathered round the wreckage his living ten team members to vote whether to "struggle or surrender". Kennedy said: "there is nothing at all the publication on circumstances in this way. A whole lot of those males have households and a few of you've got kiddies. What should you really would like to complete? I don't have anything to shed " shunning surrender, approximately 2:00 p.m. On august two, the guys sailed in direction of plum pudding island 3.5 kilometers (5.6 kilometers) south west of those stays of pt109. Irrespective of re-injuring his spine at the crash, Kennedy hammered a defectively burnt crewman throughout the drinking water into the island having a lifetime coat strap between his teeth. Kennedy forced another two-mile float at the nights august 2, 1943, to ferguson passage to make an effort to beating a departure American pt ship to reevaluate his team's rescue and experimented with create the vacation on another nighttime, at a busted kayak located on nauru island exactly where he'd swum together with ensign george ross on to search for foodstuff.

But on august 4, 1943, he along with lenny thom helped his wounded and thirsty team to a rough swim 3.75 kilometers (6.04 kilometers) south east to olasana island, that had been observable for the team out of their bare house on plum pudding isle. They drifted in opposition to a powerful current, also once-again Kennedy hammered the defectively burnt motor machinist "pappy" mcmahon with his own entire life vest. The marginally more substantial olasana island experienced mature grape bushes, however no refreshing h20. Over the subsequent evening, august 5, Kennedy and ensign george ross left the 1-hour swim into nauru island, another space of roughly.5 kilometers (0.80 kilometers) southwest, seeking assistance and foodstuff. Kennedy and ross located a tiny kayak, packs of crackers, candies along with also a fifty-gallon drum of potable water abandoned from the western, and

Kennedy paddled a second half mile straight back into olasana from the kayak to supply his famished team. Lieutenant "bud" liebe now, a companion and previous tentmate of both Kennedy's, rescued Kennedy along with his team olasana island about august 8, 1943 aboard his ship pt-157, together with all the assistance of shore watcher lieutenant reginald evans and lots of indigenous shore watchers, specially biuku gaza along with eroni kumara.

Commanding pt 59

Kennedy required just monthly to recuperate and came back into obligation, controlling the pt 59, very first eliminating the forged tubes along with thickness costs and re-fitting her one month to a significantly equipped gunboat measure two computerized 40mm firearms and 10 .50 grade browning machine guns. The aim was supposed to install 1 gunboat to just about every pt ship department in order to add weapon scope and power contrary to barges and coast ships that your 5 9 struck on a few situations in mid-october by way of mi November. About october 8, 1943, Kennedy has been encouraged to full lieutenant. About November two, Kennedy's pt59 took a part in just two additional pts at the prosperous rescue of forty --fifty marines. Even the 5 9 functioned like a defense against coast flame and shielded them since they escaped two rescue landing craft in the root of their warrior river in choiseul island, carrying eight marines aboard and bringing them into protection. Under physician's orders, Kennedy was relieved of the control of pt59 on November 18, also shipped into a healthcare facility tulagi. From that point he came back into the USA in early january 1944. Following obtaining treatment due to his back injuries, he had been discharged from active responsibility in late 1944.

Kennedy was hospitalized in the chelsea naval hospital at chelsea, Massachusetts from may to december 1944. On june 1-2 he had been presented with the navy and marine corps medal for his epic action on august 1) --two, 1943, and also the purple heart medal because of his spine accident whilst on pt109. From january 1945, Kennedy invested more months recovering out of his spine accident in castle hot springs, a hotel and non-permanent army hospital at arizona. Subsequent to the war, Kennedy believed the the trophy he'd acquired for heroism wasn't just a beat award and requested he could had been re considered to that silver star medal which he was advocated. Kennedy's daddy also asked his son have the silver star, that will be given for gallantry in actions.

But on august 1 2, 1944," Kennedy's older brother, joe jr., a pilot was murdered while devoting to get an exclusive and poisonous atmosphere assignment. His first explosive-laden airplane awakened as soon as the airplane's bombs detonated prematurely as the airplane had been flying across the english channel.

But on march 1, 1945," Kennedy retired by the navy reserve on actual handicap and has been honorably discharged with all the entire position of lieutenant. When asked how he turned into a war fanatic, Kennedy joked: "it had been uncomplicated. They minimize on my pt ship."

In 1950the division of the navy made available Kennedy a bronze star medal in recognition of the meritorious provider, and that he diminished. Kennedy's two first awards are on screen in the John f. Kennedy presidential library and museum.

Military awards

Kennedy's military awards and decorations include the navy and marine corps medal; purple heart medal; American defense service medal; American campaign medal; asiatic-pacific campaign medal with three 3⁄16" bronze celebrities; as well as the world war ii victory medal.

Earth war ii victory medal

Navy and marine corps medal citation

To get acutely epic behavior as commanding officer of motor torpedo boat 109 after collision and sinking of this boat at the pacific war location on august 1) --two, 1943. Unmindful of private threat, lieutenant (then lieutenant, junior grade) Kennedy unhesitatingly braved the dangers and dangers of shadow to lead rescue functions, swimming a long time to procure food and aid afterwards he'd triumphed in getting his crew. His superb bravery, leadership and endurance led for the rescue of a number of lives and so were commensurate with the best traditions of the united states naval services.

James forrestal, secretary of the navy

Journalism

In april 1945," Kennedy's dad, that was simply a pal of william randolph hearst, organized a stance because of his child because of distinctive correspondent for hearst newspapers; the mission stored Kennedy's identify at the eye along with "expose[d] him as a potential livelihood". He also was employed like a correspondent which may possibly, within the potsdam meeting along with different occasions.

Congressional vocation (1947--1960)

JFK's elder brother joe'd become your family's political standard bearer and'd been exploited with their own dad to look for the presidency. Joe's passing throughout the war in 1944 shifted that path and also the mission fell to JFK whilst the next oldest of their Kennedy siblings.

Residence of reps (1947--1953)

In the advocating of Kennedy's dad, U.S. Consultant james michael curley vacated his chair at the democratic 11th congressional district of Massachusetts to eventually become mayor of boston at 1946. Kennedy launched his mansion with a flat construction about 122 bowdoin avenue across in the Massachusetts statehouse. Together with his dad funding and directing his effort under the motto "the brand-new generation provides a pacesetter "," Kennedy won the democratic chief using 1 2 percentage of their vote, beating ten additional candidates. Campaigning all around boston, Kennedy known for far better home for most veterans, improved medical care for everybody, and also encourage for coordinated labour's effort for moderate work hours, even a wholesome office, and also the best way to manage, bargain, and attack. Additionally, he seeking peace throughout the un and robust resistance towards the soviet union. Nevertheless, republicans took charge of your house from the 1946 elections," Kennedy defeated his democratic rival in the election, requiring 7 3 percentage of their vote. In addition to richard nixon and joseph mccarthy, Kennedy was clearly one of many earth war ii pros chosen to congress which season.

He also functioned at your house for 2 decades, linking the powerful instruction and labor committee as well as the veterans' affairs committee. He focused his interest on worldwide events, encouraging the truman doctrine while the proper reaction to this rising cold war. He additionally encouraged public home as opposed to labor management relations act of 1947, which confined that the power of labour unions. Though much less outspoken an anti-communist since mccarthy," Kennedy affirmed the immigration and nationality act of 1952, that demanded communists to enroll using the us government, also he deplored that the "lack in china".

Having functioned being a boy scout throughout his youth, Kennedy was busy from the boston council by 1946 to 1955: district vice chairman, person in their executive board," vice-president," in addition to being a national council agent. Nearly each weekend which congress had been in session, Kennedy would return into Massachusetts to offer addresses to veteran, fraternal, and civic classes, while still maintaining a indicator card document around those who may be ideal to get a upcoming effort for state wide off ice. JFK establish a purpose of talking in most town and city in Massachusetts ahead of 1952.

Link between this 1952 U.S. Senate election in Massachusetts

Just as ancient as 1949," Kennedy commenced getting ready to conduct to the senate from 1952 in opposition to republican three-term incumbent henry cabot lodge jr. Together with all the effort motto "Kennedy is going to do more for Massachusetts". Joseph Kennedy all over again funded and handled his own son's candidacy, whilst John Kennedy's youthful brother robert Kennedy appeared as an integral part of this effort. From the presidential elections republican dwight d. Eisenhower transported Massachusetts with a perimeter of 208,000 votes but Kennedy defeated lodge by 70,000 votes to that senate seat. This calendar year, he married jacqueline bouvier.

Kennedy endorsing adlai stevenson ii to its presidential nomination in the 1956 democratic national convention at chicago

Kennedy underwent several spinal surgeries during the following couple of decades. Regularly absent in the senate that " he had been times seriously unwell and acquired catholic final rites.

Throughout his convalescence at 1956he published profiles in courage, " a publication roughly U.S. Senators who risked their own livelihood to get their own beliefs," for he won the pulitzer prize for biography in 1957. Rumors this job had been co-written by his own closing advisor and speech writer, ted sorensen, had been supported in sorensen's 2008 auto-biography.

In the beginning of his very first semester, Kennedy dedicated to Massachusetts-specific problems by devoting invoices that will aid the fishing line, fabric producing, and watch making businesses. Back in 1954," senator Kennedy voted in favor of this saint lawrence seaway that could join the excellent lakes to the atlantic ocean, even though resistance by Massachusetts politicians that contended the undertaking will cripple new england's transportation business, for example the port of boston. Three decades after, Kennedy chose a exceptional committee to pick the 5 biggest U.S. Senators ever sold thus that their portraits can beautify the senate reception space. The exact identical calendar year, Kennedy combined the senate labor rackets committee using his brother robert (who had been main adviser) to explore crime infiltration of labour unions. Back in 1958, Kennedy launched a bill (s. 3974) that became the very first big labour connections monthly bill to maneuver house as the taft hartley act of 1947. The charge dealt mainly with all the constraint of marriage abuses subjected by the mcclellan committee but failed to comprise rough taft hartley alterations asked by president eisenhower. It endured senate flooring efforts to comprise taft hartley alterations and attained passing but had been refused from your house.

Results of all Kennedy's reelection into the U.S. Senate by Massachusetts at 1958

In that the 1956 democratic party national convention," Kennedy gave the nominating address to its party's presidential nominee, adlai stevenson ii. Stevenson allow the seminar find the vice-presidential nominee. Kennedy ended 2nd in the balloting, shedding to senator estes kefauver of tennessee but acquiring federal vulnerability for a outcome.

Certainly, one of the things requiring Kennedy's awareness at the senate has been president eisenhower's charge to its civil rights act of 1957. Kennedy throw a procedural vote contrary to it, believed by some as a appeasement of both southern democratic rivals of this expenses. Kennedy failed vote title iii of this action, that could have contributed the attorney general powers to enjoin, but majority leader lyndon b. Johnson consented to enable the pro vision expire because of compromise step. Kennedy additionally voted for title iv, known as the "jury demo modification". Lots of civil rights advocates during that period criticized the expectancy as a person that could weaken the action. Your last success expenses, that Kennedy affirmed, has been passed september 1957. He suggested july two, 1957 the U.S. Service algeria's attempt to add freedom from france. This calendar year, Kennedy penned a country of immigrants (later on released in 1964), that studied the value of authorities within the united kingdom's history in addition to suggestions to reevaluate immigration legislation.

Jack par interviews senator Kennedy about the tonight show (1959)

In 1958," Kennedy was devoting to some second semester from the senate, beating republican rival, boston law firm vincent j. Celeste, with way of a gross profit of 874,608 votes, even that the most significant gross profit from the foundation of Massachusetts politics. This had been re-election effort that Kennedy's media secretary during some moment, robert e. Thompson," assemble a movie entitled the U.S. Senator John f. Kennedy tale, that displayed per day at the life span of this senator and showcased his family existence in addition to the innerworkings of his business office to fix Massachusetts-related problems. This absolutely was essentially the most in-depth picture produced roughly Kennedy up to this moment. Inside the wake of the re-election," Kennedy commenced getting ready to operate for president traveling across the U.S. With all the intent of constructing his candidacy to get 1960.

When it arrived into conservation," Kennedy, a Massachusetts audubon society supporter, desired to be certain the shorelines of cape cod stayed unsullied by prospective industrialization. On september 3, 1959," Kennedy co-sponsored that the cape cod national seashore charge together with his democratic party colleague senator leverett subtotal.

Kennedy's dad proved to be a solid supporter and pal of senator joseph mccarthy. In addition, bobby Kennedy functioned for mccarthy's sub committee, also mccarthy outdated Kennedy's sister patricia. Back in 1954, the senate voted to censure mccarthy, also Kennedy drafted a language encouraging the censure. But it wasn't delivered as Kennedy was hospitalized during the moment; point. The address placed Kennedy at the obvious location of engaging by "matching" his vote towards this of the other senator, also conflicting the censure. Even though Kennedy never ever signaled he would have resolved, the incident harmed his aid members of their liberal area, for example eleanor roosevelt, from the 1956 and 1960 elections.

Chapter two
1960 presidential election

But on december 17, 1959, a correspondence by Kennedy's team who has been sent to both "busy and powerful democrats" was leaked saying he would announce his presidential effort january 2, 1960. On january 2, 1960, Kennedy declared his candidacy for the democratic party presidential nomination. While many contested Kennedy's experience and age, his charm and eloquence left him multiple fans. Most people in America held anti-catholic attitudes, but Kennedy's outspoken help of this separation of state and church served defuse the circumstance. His faith also aided him to triumph a committed following one of lots of catholic republicans. Kennedy confronted several prospective challengers for the democratic party nomination, such as senate majority leader lyndon b. Johnson, adlai stevenson ii, also senator hubert humphrey.

Kennedy's presidential effort has been a family affair," financed with his own dad along his brother robert, behaving like his own campaign director. John favored ivy league coverage advisers, however with his own dad he experienced the give and get of Massachusetts politics and also assembled in predominantly irish group of campaigners, led by larry o'brien along with kenneth o'donnell. Kennedy traveled widely to assemble his service one of democratic elites and republicans. At time, get together officials commanded nearly all of their delegates, however, a few nations also held primaries, also Kennedy hunted to acquire a few primaries to raise his opportunities winning the nomination. In his very first big evaluation, Kennedy won the wisconsin first, effortlessly finishing humphrey's hopes of winning the presidency. None the less, Kennedy and humphrey confronted each other at an aggressive west virginia leader where Kennedy couldn't gain by the catholic bloc, " as he'd in wisconsin. Kennedy won the west virginia first, impressing quite a few at the get together, however in the beginning of this 1960 democratic party national convention, it had been unsure concerning if he'd win against the nomination.

Full broadcast of this initial nationwide televised presidential argument

When Kennedy entered the seminar that he had probably the maximum delegates, however perhaps not sufficient to make sure he would gain the nomination. Stevenson--both the 1952 and 1956 presidential nominee--stayed quite popular inside the social gathering, whilst Johnson also expected to acquire against the nomination using the aid from party leaders. Kennedy's candidacy additionally confronted resistance by previous president harry s. Truman, that was simply concerned with Kennedy's insufficient encounter. Kennedy realized a second ballot will grant the nomination into Johnson or somebody else," along with also his well-organized effort surely could bring in the aid of only enough delegates to get the presidential nomination to the very first ballot.

Kennedy disregarded the resistance of his own brother, who also needed him to select labor leader walter reuther, and also different liberal fans if he picked Johnson as his vice-presidential nominee. He considered the Texas senator will help him acquire support by your south. [105] the option infuriated numerous in labour. Alf cio president george meany named Johnson "the arch-foe of work," whilst illinois afl cio president reuben soderstrum claimed Kennedy experienced "forced chumps from frontrunners of their American labour movement" despite accepting the nomination, Kennedy gave his most renowned "new frontier" address, expressing, "for that issues aren't all resolved and also the conflicts aren't all won--and also we endure now around the boundary of the new frontier. ... However, the new frontier of which i speak isn't some claims --this really is a pair of struggles. It sums up not exactly what i mean to offer you the American folks, however, exactly what i mean to request for them"

In the beginning of fall general election effort, republican nominee and vice president richard nixon maintained that a six-point direct from the surveys. [109] important problems included ways exactly to find the market moving Kennedy's roman catholicism, " the Cuban revolution, and also perhaps the distance and missile plans of this soviet union experienced exceeded those of their U.S. To tackle anxieties his getting catholic will impression his decision, he told the greater houston ministerial association on september 1 2, 1960:"i'm not the catholic candidate for president. I'm the democratic party candidate for president that happens to become catholic. I don't really speak for my church on public affairs --and also the church will not talk " Kennedy asked rhetorically if one quarter of Americans ended up sentenced into second-class citizenship simply because these certainly were catholic, also when said that"[n]o you requested me my own faith [functioning the navy] from the south pacific".

Document: usg-1-w excerpt - John f. Kennedy and jacqueline Kennedy vote election deworm

Kennedy and his spouse jacqueline vote in boston on election-day

Between september and october, Kennedy withdrew from nixon in the very first televised presidential discussions at U.S. Heritage. Over the apps, nixon experienced a wounded leg"5 o'clock shadow", also has been perspiring, which makes him search uncomfortable and stressed. Unexpectedly, Kennedy wore cosmetics and also seemed peaceful, which aided the huge tv viewer to look at him because the winner. Normally radio listeners believed nixon had won that the disagreements ended up a lure. [112] the arguments have become thought of a landmark in western ideology --that the idea in that the medium of television begun to perform with a leading part in politics.

1960 electoral election outcomes

Kennedy's campaign gained momentum following the very first argument, also then he pulled marginally before nixon generally in the majority of polls. About election day, Kennedy defeated nixon in a few of those nearest presidential elections of this 20thcentury. From the federal popular vote by many reports, Kennedy directed nixon by only two-tenths of 1 percentage (49.7percent to 49.5percent), whilst at the electoral college that he gained 303 votes to nixon's 219 (269 ended up had to triumph). Fourteen electors out of mississippi and alabama denied to encourage Kennedy due to his service to the civil rights movements; they hunted senator harry f. Byrd of virginia, as failed an elector out of oklahoma. [113] Kennedy became the youngest man (43) at any time picked into the presidency, nevertheless theodore roosevelt had been younger in 42 if he mechanically assumed that the business office following william mckinley's assassination in 1901.

Presidency (1961--1963)

Chief justice earl warren oversees the oath of office to John f. Kennedy in the capitol, january 20, 1961.

John f. Kennedy was sworn in as the 35th president in noon on january 20, 1961. Inside his inaugural speech he talked of this demand for most Americans to be more active citizens, famously stating, "ask not what your country can do to you personally. Ask exactly what you could do to help the nation " he also asked that the states of this entire world to combine with each other to battle what he termed the "common enemies of man: tyranny, poverty, and illness, and war ". He included:

"each of that won't be completed at the first fourteen times. Nor is it completed in the first one thoUSAnd days, nor at the life span with the administration, nor even perhaps in our life on the particular planet. But allow us to start" in final he enlarged upon his urge to have increased internationalism: "ultimately, if you are citizens of America or citizens of earth, ask of us the exact same high standards of energy and sacrifice that we request of you personally "

Even the address revealed Kennedy's self-confidence his government might graph a significant path in the national policy and international issues. The comparison among this positive eyesight and also the pressures of handling every day political truths in the home and overseas are among the primary anxieties running during early years of the government.

Kennedy talking at rice university at houston on september 1 2, 1962. Vice president lyndon b. Johnson may be understood at the rear of him.

Kennedy attracted into this whitehouse a comparison in company in comparison to this conclusion arrangement of former-general eisenhower, also he lost time at scrapping eisenhower's techniques. Kennedy chosen the organizational arrangement of the wheel along with all the current spokes causing the president. He had been prepared and ready to really make the higher variety of fast decisions demanded within this kind of ecosystem. He also selected a blend of inexperienced and experienced individuals to function in his cupboard. "we could find our tasks collectively", " he said.

Far into the chagrin of his own economic advisers, that needed him to lose taxation, Kennedy immediately decided into your balanced financial assurance. That has been had in market for votes to further enlarge the membership of their house rules committee as a way to provide the democrats many in establishing the legislative schedule. The president centered on instantaneous and special topics dealing with the government and immediately lent his impatience with thinking of deeper significance. Deputy national security advisor walt whitman rostow as soon as commenced a diatribe regarding the rise of communism, also Kennedy unexpectedly cut off him, inquiring, "what can you really need me to take action this now?"

Kennedy approved protection secretary robert mcnamara's contentious choice to award the agreement to its f 111 tfx (tactical fighter experimental) fighter bomber into standard dynamics (that the selection of the civilian surveillance division) more than boeing (that the option of the armed forces). In the request of senator henry jackson," senator John mcclellan held 4 6 times of primarily closed-door hearings before the permanent subcommittee on investigations exploring the tfx deal out of february to November 1963.

Throughout the summertime of 1962, Kennedy needed a covert taping technique place in the white house, many likely to assist his upcoming memoir. It listed many discussions with Kennedy along with his cabinet members, for example people in connection with this "Cuban missile crisis".

Overseas coverage

President Kennedy's foreign policy has been dominated by American confrontations with the soviet union, exemplified by proxy competitions at early period of this cold war. Back in 1961 he anticipated a summit with soviet premier nikita khrushchev. He started out to the inappropriate foot by responding aggressively into some regular khrushchev address on cold war confrontation at early-1961. The address was first created for national audiences from the soviet union, but Kennedy translated it for your own struggle. His fault helped increase anxieties going in the vienna summit of june 1961.

But on how into this summit, Kennedy ceased in paris to meet up with french president charles de gaulle, who counseled him to discount khrushchev's fresh personality. The french president emphasized the USA' supposed sway in europe. Yet, de gaulle was impressed with all the youthful president along with his family. Kennedy picked on this in his own address at paris, expressing he would be recalled as "the guy who followed jackie Kennedy into paris".

Even the kekkonen's out of finland seen the united states of America and fulfilled John f. Kennedy in 1961. From left president urho kekkonen," sylvie kekkonen, jacqueline Kennedy onassis, and John f. Kennedy.

But on june 4, 1961, the president satisfied with khrushchev at vienna and abandoned handed the meetings mad and frustrated he'd permitted the highest to frighten him despite the warnings he'd obtained. Khrushchev, because of his role, was amazed with all the president intellect, however, assumed him feeble. Kennedy did triumph in distributing the lowest lineup to khrushchev to the very sensitive dilemma, " a projected treaty between moscow and east berlin. He left it crystal clear any treaty interfering together with U.S. Accessibility legal rights west berlin will be considered an act of warfare.

Fleetingly subsequent to the president came back household, " the U.S.s.r. Introduced its own plan to sign a treaty with east-berlin, abrogating any third-party job legal rights in the industry of their metropolis. Depressed and upset, Kennedy supposed his sole solution was supposed to ready the united states for atomic warfare, he thought experienced a one-in-five likelihood of transpiring.

Kennedy using kwame nkrumah, the very first thoughts of a different ghana, march 1961

Kennedy with all the prime minister amin tore fanfan, in the whitehouse, at 1963

In the months immediately after vienna summit, even significantly more than 20,000 individuals returned from east berlin into the western industry, responding to announcements against your U.S.s.r. Kennedy commenced intensive conferences around the berlin dilemma, at which dean acheson chose the lead to advocating a military buildup alongside nato allies. Within an july 1961 address, Kennedy introduced his choice to put in $3.25 billion (comparable to $27.81 billion in 20-19) into this shield funding, and above 200,000 other troops," saying an assault on west berlin will be obtained within a attack about the

U.S. The address obtained an 85% approval score.

Even a month afterwards, the soviet union and also east-berlin commenced blocking further passing through of east berliners to west berlin and built barbed wire fences around the metropolis, that were immediately updated towards the berlin wall. Kennedy's original response was supposed to discount that, provided that complimentary entry by west to east berlin ongoing. The class had been modified once west berliners had misplaced confidence at the protection in these standing from the states. Kennedy delivered vice-president Johnson, together side a lot of army employees, at convoy throughout west germany, for example soviet-armed check-points, to establish the continuing devotion of their U.S. Into west berlin.

Kennedy gave a language in saint anselm college on may 5, 1960, seeing America's behavior from the rising cold war. The speech detail by detail just how a foreign policy needs to be run in direction of african states, imagining that a sign of service to modern african American nationalism by declaring, "for people, also, based a brand-new state on re-volt from colonial rule"

Cuba and also the bay of pigs invasion

Even the eisenhower government had established a strategy to overthrow fidel castro's regime in Cuba. Directed from the central intelligence agency (cia), with assistance from this U.S. Army, the strategy was to get the invasion of Cuba using a counterrevolutionary insurgency consisting of U.S.-trained," anti-castro Cuban exiles headed by cia paramilitary officials. The aim was supposed to invade Cuba and instigate an uprising one of the Cuban men and women, expecting to eliminate castro out of power. Kennedy declared the last invasion anticipate april 4, 1961.

Even the president and vice-president walking around white house grounds

Even the bay of pigs invasion started on april 17, 1961. Fifteen-hundred U.S.-trained Cubans, dubbed brigade 2506, landed around the staircase. No more U.S. Atmosphere service has been furnished. Cia director allen dulles later on said they considered the president could get some other actions which has been desired for victory the moment the soldiers were about a lawn.

From april 1 9, 1961, the Cuban authorities had seized or murdered the invading exiles, also Kennedy had been made to negotiate for your launch of their 1,189 lands. 20 months after, Cuba published the seized exiles in exchange for $53 million worth of drug and food. The episode compelled castro really feel alert to this U.S. And directed him to feel another invasion could occur.

Biographer richard reeves reported that Kennedy concentrated largely around the political consequences of this master plan as opposed to military issues. As it was ineffective, he had been convinced the master plan has been a set to force him appear awful. He'd responsibility to its collapse, declaring, "we now got a significant kick at the leg plus also we deserved it. But possibly we will find something out of this " he made robert Kennedy to simply help direct a questionnaire to inspect the sources for the collapse.

In late-1961, the white house shaped the exceptional group (augmented), led by robert Kennedy and which include edward lansdale," secretary robert mcnamara, along with also others. The band's aim --to overthrow castro by way of espionage, sabotage, and also other secret approaches --has been not chased.

Cuban missile crisis

Cuban missile crisis

But on oct 14, 1962, cia u2 spy planes took images of their soviets' structure of intermediate-range ballistic missile sites in Cuba. The pics were first demonstrated to Kennedy on october 16; a consensus has been reached since the missiles had been also offensive in character and ergo introduced a direct nuclear menace.

Kennedy faced an issue: in case the U.S. Assaulted the sites, then it may possibly cause atomic war with all the U.S.s.r., however when the U.S. Did nothing whatsoever, it'd have to deal with all the higher danger from close-range atomic firearms. Even the U.S. Would likewise appear into this entire world as significantly less devoted into this safety of this volcano. Over a certain point, Kennedy had to demonstrate fix in a reaction to khrushchev, notably soon after the vienna summit.

Soviet leading nikita khrushchev and Kennedy confer in vienna, 1961

Longer compared to a 3rd of U.S. National security council (nsc) associates preferred that an unannounced air attack on the missile websites, however to get several of these conjured an image of "pearl harbor backwards". There has been also some problem against the global group (questioned in optimism), which the attack plan has been still an overreaction in light to this simple fact eisenhower experienced set pgm-19 jupiter missiles from italy and turkey at 1958. Additionally, it wouldn't be able to rest certain the attack could be 100 percent more effective. Back in concurrence using a majority-vote of this nsc," Kennedy chose in the naval quarantine. On october 22he published an email into khrushchev and introduced your choice on television.

Even the U.S. Navy will discontinue and scrutinize each of soviet boats coming off Cuba, commencing october 2 4. The business of American states gave unanimous support towards the elimination of their missiles. The president traded two collections of letters together with khrushchev, without avail. Un (un) secretary general u-thant asked each function to undo their own conclusions and also input into a cooling-off period of time. Khrushchev consented, however, Kennedy failed to.

Certainly, one soviet-flagged boat was discontinued and stopped. On october 28, khrushchev agreed to dismantle the missile websites, susceptible to un reviews. Even the U.S. Openly claimed to not invade Cuba and independently consented to clear away its jupiter missiles out of italy and turkey, that were then obsolete and'd been supplanted by submarines armed with ugm-27 polaris missiles.

This catastrophe caused the world closer to nuclear war than anytime just before or later. It's regarded that "the humankind" of khrushchev and Kennedy prevailed. The catastrophe enhanced the picture of willpower and also the president's authenticity. Kennedy's acceptance ranking climbed from 66 percent to 77% instantly afterwards.

Latin America and also communism

Kennedy within an official trip together with chilean president jorge alessandria," december 1962

Believing who "people who make peaceful revolution impossible, will make violent revolution inevitable, even" Kennedy sought to retain the perceived risk of communism from latin America by setting the alliance for progress, which sent aid for a state and sought greater human rights criteria within the area. He worked closely together with puerto rican governor luis muñoz marín to its evolution of this alliance of improvement, also started functioning toward puerto rico's liberty.

Even the eisenhower government, throughout the cia, had started formulating strategies to assassinate castro from Cuba and also rafael trujillo in the dominican republic. After president Kennedy took office," he educated the cia any approach has to consist of plausible deniability from the U.S. His general public standing has been in resistance. Back in june 1961, the dominican republic's chief was imprisoned; at today after, undersecretary of state chester bowles headed a careful response from the country. Robert Kennedy, that watched a chance for this U.S., referred to as bowles "that a gutless bastard" into his head.

Peace corps

In one among the very first presidential actions, Kennedy requested congress to generate the most peace corps. His first brother-in-law," sargent shriver, was its very first manager. Through the application, Americans offered to support growing countries in areas such as farming, education, healthcare, and structure. The company climbed to 5,000 associates from march 1963 and also 10,000 annually afterwards. Since 1961, in excess of 200,000 Americans have joined the peace corps, re-presenting 139 distinct nations.

South-east asia

Dinah diem, reaction into the 1963 south Vietnamese coup, cable 243, buddhist catastrophe, thich quang duc, xá lợi pagoda raids, krulak mendenhall assignment, also mcnamara taylor assignment

Just as a U.S. Senator at 1956," Kennedy openly urged for larger U.S. Participation in Vietnam. [162][163] after briefing Kennedy, eisenhower highlighted the greek danger in southeast-asia demanded concern; eisenhower believed laos to function as "the cork in the jar" about the regional hazard. Back in march 1961, Kennedy uttered an alteration in plan from encouraging a "complimentary" laos into some "impartial" laos, signaling privately that Vietnam, also maybe not laos, ought to be termed the USA's trip-wire to get communism's spread while in the place. In might, he freed lyndon Johnson to fulfill with south Vietnamese president ngo dinh diem. Johnson promised diem further assistance to mold a fighting power which will withstand the communists. Kennedy declared a reversal of coverage out of service to venture with diem to conquer communism from south Vietnam.

Throughout his presidency, Kennedy continuing policies which contributed political, economic, and military service for the authorities of south korea and south Vietnam.

All of us possess one million Americans now serving beyond the united states. There is absolutely no other region ever sold that has carried this type of the weight reduction. Additional nations experienced compels functioning out their country, except also for conquest. We got just two branches in south korea and never to restrain south korea, yet to shield it. We've got a whole lot of most Americans from south viet nam. No additional country on earth has done that because the start of the entire world; greece, rome, napoleon, and also the remainder, consistently experienced conquest. We've got a thoUSAnd men out, plus so they strive to shield all these nations.

In late 1961, the viet cong started imagining a overriding existence, and in the beginning seizing the provincial capital of phuoc vinh. Kennedy raised the number of military advisors and exceptional powers inside your community, from 11,000 from 1962 into 16,000 by late 1963, but he had been loath to dictate a full-blown installation of troops. Annually after 3 weeks after on march 8, 1965, his successor, president lyndon Johnson, dedicated to the very first battle troops to Vietnam and escalated U.S. Participation, together with compels achieving 184,000 annually and also 536,000 at 1968.

In overdue 1961, president Kennedy delivered roger hillman, subsequently manager of the state department's bureau of intelligence and investigation, to appraise the specific situation in Vietnam. There, hillman fulfilled sir robert grainger ker thompson and head of the british advisory mission into south viet nam, and also the strategic hamlet program has been shaped. This had been accepted by Kennedy and south Vietnam president ngo dinh diem. This absolutely was executed at ancient 1962 and entailed a few driven moves, village internment, along with segregation of rural south Vietnamese in to fresh communities through which in fact the peasantry is dispersed out of communist insurgents. It had been estimated these brand-new communities could offer safety for those peasants and fortify the link between the fundamental federal government. From November 1963the app and formally stopped in 1964.

In ancient 1962, Kennedy officially approved in-state involvement after he first signed up the national security action memorandum -- "subversive insurgency (battle of liberation)". "operation ranch hand", a largescale aerial defoliation campaign, began around the roadsides of both south Vietnams. Based upon that examination Kennedy approved (office of defense or state) there had been no or small advancement in simplifying the rise in greek aggression in yield to an enlarged U.S. Participation.

Kennedy with prospective australian prime minister harold holt at the oval office at 1963

In april 1963," Kennedy evaluated the position in Vietnam, declaring, "we do not have a prayer of residing in Vietnam. People folks despise us. They truly are planning to to throw out our asses from there in any given point. I, however, cannot stop trying this land towards the communists and find the American individuals to reelect me"

But on august 2-1, as the brand-new U.S. Ambassador henry cabot lodge jr. Came, diem and his brother ngo dinh nhu requested south Vietnam forces, both financed and trained by the cia, to quell buddhist demonstrations. Even the crack-downs increased expectations of the coup d'état to take away diem with (or by) his brother, nhu. Lodge has been taught to decide to try becoming diem and nhu to measure back and depart the nation. Diem would perhaps not hear lodge. Cable 243 (deptel 243) adopted dated august 2 4, announcing washington wouldn't longer endure nhu's activities, also lodge has been arranged to strain diem to get rid of nhu.

Lodge reasoned the sole choice was supposed to find the south Vietnamese generals to overthrow diem and nhu. At week's end, orders had been shipped to saigon and around washington to "damage all coup wires". At an identical period, the very first proper anti-Vietnam warfare belief was voiced by U.S. Clergy in your ministers' Vietnam committee.

Even a whitehouse assembly in september was due to those distinct ongoing assessments; the president has been awarded upgraded examinations after private testimonials about the earth from the departments of protection (common victor krulak) and condition (joseph mendenhall). Krulak reported the armed forces struggle the communists was progressing and also being obtained, whereas mendenhall said the nation has been lost into some U.S. Have an effect on. Kennedy responded, inquiring, "can you gentlemen see precisely the exact same nation?" the president has been oblivious which each man ended up in such chances they hadn't talked to one another in the return excursion.

In oct 1963, the president named defense secretary mcnamara and general maxwell d. Taylor into some civic assignment in a second attempt to populate with the formulation and information of coverage. The goal of this mcnamara taylor assignment "highlighted the value of becoming into the base of the the gaps in coverage by U.S. Agents in viet nam". According to mcnamara, taylor, and lodge, diem repeatedly refused to concur on regulating steps, assisting dispel mcnamara's preceding optimism about diem. Taylor and mcnamara have been educated by Vietnam's vice president," nguyen ngoc tho (range of all to triumph diem), that in detail by detail phrases obliterated taylor's advice the armed forces was success from the countryside. In Kennedy's insistence, the assignment contained in planned program for troop entry: 1000 by the year's ending and total withdrawal from 1965, something that the nsc believed for "tactical dream".

In late oct, intellect cables reported a coup from the diem administration was afoot. The origin, spartan common duong van minh (known as "big minh"), desired to be aware of that the U.S. Placement. Kennedy educated lodge to provide essential aid into the coup, including assassination. About November 1, 1963," south Vietnamese generals, headed by "big minh", overthrew the diem authorities, arresting then killing diem and nhu. Kennedy was amazed with the fatalities.

News of those coups contributed to revived confidence --each in the us as well as in south Vietnam--which the war may possibly be won. Mcgeorge bundy drafted a national protection motion memo to gift to Kennedy up on his return out of Dallas. It revealed that the work to resist communism in Vietnam, together with rising military and financial help and enlargement of functions to laos and cambodia. Prior to making for Dallas," Kennedy informed michael forrestal who "following first of this 12 months... [he wished] a comprehensive analysis of just about every potential selection, for example ways to make out from there... To critique the complete thing by the floor into the upper". When asked what he imagined the president supposed, forrestal mentioned, "it had been devil's impulse stuff"

Kennedy supplies the commencement address in American university, june 10, 1963

Historians disagree on perhaps the Vietnam war might have escalated if Kennedy had been assassinated and'd won reelection at 1964. Fueling the argument were announcements created from secretary of defense mcnamara from the movie "the fog of war" which Kennedy was considering yanking on the united states of America from Vietnam following the 1964 election.

The movie also comprises a cassette
lyndon Johnson saying that Ker
intending to draw a spot where Johnse
disagreed. Kennedy had signed national security
action memorandum (nsam) 263, dated oct 1-1,
that arranged the withdrawal from 1000 military
employees at the year's ending, and also the
almost all these outsides by 1965. This kind of act
might have turned into an insurance policy
modification; however, Kennedy had been openly
proceeding at a hawkish management
considering that his address in the world serenity
in American university on june 10, 1963.

In the period of Kennedy's departure, no last plan
decision was first forced to Vietnam. Back in 2008
theodore sorensen composed, "i'd love to feel that
Kennedy might have observed a means to draw
all of American teachers and advisers [out of
Vietnam]. However, ... I don't actually consider he
realized from his past weeks that which he had
been about to complete " sorensen included , in

his own ruling, Vietnam "was not the only real foreign coverage difficulty handed by JFK into his successor in no more and worse, contour when it had been once he inherited it" U.S. Participation from the field dove before his successor lyndon Johnson straight deployed routine U.S. Army forces for battling with the Vietnam war. Right after Kennedy's assassination, president Johnson signed nsam 273 on November 26, 1963. It hastens Kennedy's conclusion to draw 1000 troops, also reaffirmed the coverage of guidance into this south Vietnamese.

American college address

World peace speech

Even a plan of peace

On june 10, 1963, Kennedy, in the top point of the rhetorical powers, given the commencement speech at American university at washington, d.c.

Additionally referred as "a plan of ", maybe not did the president outline a strategy to curtail atomic arms but he "laid outside.

Paradoxically, yet realistic path for earth peace in some period whenever the U.S. And also soviet union confronted the prospect of an escalating nuclear weapons race" the president wanted:

To go over an issue about which overly usually ignorance abounds and the truth is far too rarely sensed --nonetheless it's by far the most essential topic in the world: earth peace... I talk about peace on account of the newest experience of warfare... Within a era every time a mythical atomic weapon comprises 10 times the explosive force delivered by the allied powers at the next world war... An era whenever the deadly poisons produced by a nuclear exchange will be transported by wind and atmosphere and dirt and seed to the far corners of the world and to generations yet unborn... I talk about peace, so, while the necessary rational end of rational males... Globe peace, like community peace, will not necessitate that every man love his neighbor--it requires just they reside with each other in reciprocal tolerance... Our issues are somewhat artificial --hence they are sometimes solved by man. And man is frequently as massive as he needs.

Even the president left 2 statements: 1).) The soviets had voiced a urge to negotiate with a nuclear test ban treaty, also two) the U.S. Experienced postponed intended atmospheric evaluations.

West berlin address

Kennedy delivering his address west berlin

In 1963, germany was putting up with some period of specific exposure as a result of soviet aggression into the east and the imminent retirement of west german chancellor adenauer. At an identical period, french president charles de gaulle was attempting to construct a franco-west german counter-weight into the soviet and American spheres of influence. On Kennedy's eyes," that this franco-german alliance seemed led at nato's sway in europe.

But on june 26," president Kennedy gave a public address in west berlin. He whined the American devotion to germany and criticized communism, also has been met by having the ecstatic answer by a gigantic crowd. Kennedy used the building of the berlin wall for instance of the failures of communism:" freedom has many troubles, and democracy isn't best. However, we've not needed to place a wall around continue to keep us, to keep them from departing us" the address has been well known for the famous phrase "ich bin ein berliner" ("i'm a citizen of berlin"). Some thoUSAnd individuals were about the avenue to get its address. Kennedy commented to ted sorensen later: "we will do not have one more afternoon just like that particular one, for as long as we all live.

Israel

In 1960," Kennedy said, "israel will flourish and endure. It's the baby of the residence of the brave. It could neither be broken by adversity nor demoralized by success. It carries the shield of democracy and it honors the sword of liberty "

Just as president," Kennedy pioneered the production of protection ties with israel, also he's blamed as the creator of their us-israeli army cooperation, that may be ongoing below following presidents. Kennedy stopped the arms embargo the eisenhower and truman administrations experienced enforced israel. Assessing the security of israel because of national and ethical devotion, he had been the very first ever to present the idea of the "exclusive relationship" (because he explained it into golda meir) involving your USA and israel.

Kennedy together with israeli foreign minister golda meir," december 27, 1962

Kennedy extended the initial informal stability promises to israel from 1962 as well as from 1963, has been the very first us president to enable the sale to israel of sophisticated us weaponry (that the mim-23 hawk) and to supply diplomatic support for israeli procedures, that were compared by arab neighbors; these coverages comprised israel's drinking water endeavor onto the jordan river.

Just as a consequence with the freshly produced security cooperation, Kennedy additionally struck worries with all the israeli govt across the creation of atomic substances in dimona, which he considered might instigate a nuclear arms race from the middle east. Subsequent to the presence of the nuclear plant had been denied by the israeli authorities, david ben gurion said in a language into the israeli knesset on december 2 1, 1960, which the intention behind the atomic plant in beersheba was to get "exploration in issues of arctic desert and zones fauna and flora". After ben gurion fulfilled with Kennedy at nyc, he maintained that dimona was developed to supply atomic power to get de-salinization along with other peaceful reasons "for now being".

In 1963 that the Kennedy government was participated in a currently declassified diplomatic standoff with all the israel. At a mighty 1963 correspondence into ben-gurion," Kennedy wrote he had been doubtful and also said that American aid to israel would possibly be in danger if reputable details regarding the israeli atomic program wasn't coming, ben gurion replicated preceding reassurances which dimona had been being made for peaceful reasons. The israeli govt resisted American pressure to start its own atomic facilities to international atomic energy agency (iaea) inspections. Back in 1962 the united states and israeli authorities had decided to a yearly scrutiny regimen. A science attaché in the embassy at telavi reasoned that portions of this dimona center was closed down to deceive scientists whenever they seen.

Based into seymour hersh, the israelis setup fictitious hands chambers to demonstrate that the us citizens. Israeli lobbyist abe feinberg said: "it had been a portion of the occupation to trick off them that Kennedy was insisting on [a review]. " hersh asserts the testimonials were ran within a way that it "ensured the entire procedure will be more than the usual white wash, since the president along with his most senior advisers experienced to comprehend the American review group would need to program its visits properly beforehand, along with the entire acquiescence of both israel." marc trachtenberg contended that"[a]although [he had been] aware of the israelis ended up doing," Kennedy decided to accept action satisfactory evidence of israeli compliance together with the USA's nonproliferation policy" [224] " the American who headed the review team said the critical objective of the inspections would be to locate "approaches to perhaps not get to the purpose of carrying action from israel's atomic weapons software".

Rodger davies, the manager of this state dept's office of near eastern affairs, reasoned in march 1965 which israel was growing atomic weapons. He declared that israel's goal date for accomplishing nuclear functionality was 1968--1969. On may 1), 1968," undersecretary of state nicholas katzenbach instructed president Johnson the dimona was creating sufficient plutonium to develop two bombs per calendar year. Even the state department contended when israel required arms, then it will acknowledge international oversight of its own atomic regime. Dimona wasn't placed directly under iaea safeguards. Efforts to compose israeli adherence to the atomic nonproliferation treaty (npt) in to contracts to its distribution of U.S. Firearms lasted through the duration of 1968.

Iraq

Relations amongst the USA and also iraq became entangled after overthrow of their iraqi monarchy about july 14, 1958," which led to the announcement of some republican federal government headed by brigadier abd al-karim qassim. On june 25, 1961, qassim mobilized troops over the boundary between iraq and kuwait, announcing the latter state "an integral portion of iraq" and inducing a shortlived"kuwait crisis". The great britain --that had only allowed kuwait liberty on june 1 9, also whose market has been heavily reliant on kuwaiti petroleum -- reacted to july inch from alerting 5,000 troops into the united states to dissuade an iraqi invasion. At an identical period, Kennedy discharged a U.S.

Navy taskforce to bahrain, and also the united kingdom (in the advocating of this Kennedy government) attracted the emptiness to united nations security council, at which in fact the projected settlement was vetoed from the soviet union. The specific situation has been solved in october, whenever the british soldiers had been removed and substituted with a 4,000-strong arab league pressure.

In december 1961," qassim's authorities passed public-law eighty, that confined that the british-and also American-owned iraq petroleum company (ipc)'s concessionary carrying into all those areas at which oil has been being generated, effortlessly expropriating 99.5percent of those ipc concession. U.S. Officers were alerted from the expropriation in addition to the new soviet union of an egyptian-sponsored un resolution asking the admittance of both kuwait because un member nation, they considered were all also connected. Senior national security council advisor robert kamer feared when the ipc stopped production at reaction, qassim could "catch kuwait" (so accomplishing a "strangle hold" on middle eastern oil creation) or even "toss himself to russian arms". Kamer additionally produced be aware of rumors a civic coup in opposition to qassim would possibly be impending, also had the capacity to "put iraq back again [a] a lot more impartial keel".

In april 1962, the state department issued fresh tips about iraq which were meant to raise American sway. Meanwhile, the Kennedy educated the cia--beneath the leadership of archibald bulloch roosevelt jr.--to get started making preparations for a military coup from qassim.

Even the anti-imperialist and also anticommunist iraqi ba'ath party overthrew and implemented qassim at a barbarous coup on february 8, 1963. Whilst there were rumors which the cia orchestrated the coup, declassified files along with also the testimony of former cia officials imply there wasn't any immediate American participation, even though cia was seeking a ideal replacement qassim over the iraqi armed forces and'd been advised of a previous ba'athist coup plot. Even the Kennedy government was satisfied about the effect and finally permitted a 55-million arms bargain for iraq.

Ireland

Kennedy visiting the John barry memorial in crescent quay at wexford, ireland

President Kennedy at motorcade at patrick road, cork, in ireland on june 28, 1963

Throughout his inaugural trip for his ancestral dwelling of ireland at june 1963," [2 3 4] Kennedy recognized a grant of armorial bearings by the main herald of ireland and received honorary degrees from the national university of ireland and trinity college, dublin. [235] he visited with the cabin at dungan town, nearby new ross, county wexford, at which his ancestors had dwelt just before emigrating to the us.

Kennedy was that the very first international leader to deal with homes of the oireachtas (the irish parliament). On december 22, 2006, the irish office of justice published declassified police records suggesting that stability had been increased since Kennedy had been that the niche of about three passing dangers in that trip.

Nuclear-test-ban treaty

President Kennedy signals the partial test ban treaty, a significant landmark in ancient atomic disarmament from the atomic age

Troubled from the long-term risks of radioactive contamination and nuclear weapons proliferation,

Kennedy and khrushchev consented to sue with a nuclear test ban treaty, formerly conceived in adlai stevenson's 1956 democratic effort. Inside their vienna summit meeting in june 1961, both khrushchev and Kennedy both equally attained an everyday knowing against atomic screening, nevertheless the soviet union commenced analyzing atomic weapons september. In conclusion, the USA ran evaluations five times after. Briefly after, fresh U.S. Satellites commenced delivering pictures which managed to get crystal clear the soviets have been much supporting the U.S. From the arms race. But the atomic energy of this U.S. Has been of minor importance provided that the U.S.s.r. Sensed itself to be in parity.

In july 1963, Kennedy delivered w. Averell harriman into moscow to negotiate a treaty with the soviets. The launching sessions comprised khrushchev, who later on assigned soviet representation into andrei gromyko. It became evident a in depth evaluation ban wouldn't be executed, thanks largely into this hesitation of this soviets allowing certificates which could affirm compliance.

Fundamentally, that the united states of America, the united kingdom, as well as the soviet union were the first signatories into your constrained treaty, which prohibited atomic testing on earth, at the air, or submerged, however, maybe underground. The U.S. Senate ratified that and Kennedy signed it in october 1963. France has been swift to announce it absolutely was liberated to keep on testing and developing its own atomic defenses.

National coverage

President Kennedy at fort worth, Texas, on friday afternoon, November 22, 1963, the time of the assassination.

Kennedy termed his national app that the "new frontier". It ambitiously promised federal funds for schooling, healthcare for its older, economical help to metropolitan locations, and federal government intervention to prevent the downturn. In addition, he promised a limit to racial discrimination," however his schedule, that comprised the acceptance of this voter education project (vep) at 1962, developed modest advancement in parts like mississippi, at which in actuality the"vep reasoned that discrimination had been entrenched".

In his own 1963 condition of this union speech he suggested considerable tax reform and also a decrease in sales tax prices by the present assortment of 20--90 percent to some collection of both 14--65 percent together with a decline in the business taxation rates by 52 to 47 percent. Kennedy added the most notable speed ought to be put at 70 percent if particular obligations weren't expunged for high-income earners.

Congress failed to behave right up until 1964, a year following his departure when the top-rated individual charge was decreased into 70 percent, and also the top-rated company speed was put in 48 percent.

On that the economic club of new yorkhe talked in 1963 of"... The fact that tax prices are excessively much and earnings too reduced; and also the quickest way to increase revenue within the very long run would be to lessen rates " congress handed handful of Kennedy's leading apps throughout his life, but did vote through in 1964 and 1965 underneath his successor Johnson.

Market

Kennedy ended a span of restricted financial guidelines, loosening fiscal plan to maintain down interest rates and also to encourage progress of this market. He presided over the very first administration funding to high the 100 million mark," in 1962, along with also his very first funding in 1961 triggered the country's very first non-war," non-recession shortage. The market, that have been recessions in 3 decades and has been when Kennedy took office, hastened especially all through his government. Despite minimal inflation and rates of interest, the gdp had increased by a mean of just 2.2percent yearly throughout the eisenhower government (hardly a lot more than population increase during the period), also it'd decreased by 1 percent throughout eisenhower's past 12 weeks at workplace.

Even the market turned out and prosper throughout Kennedy's several years since president. Even the gdp expanded by a mean of 5.5percent from early-1961 into late-1963, whilst inflation stayed stable in approximately 1 percent and unemployment soared. Industrial manufacturing climbed by 15 percent and automobile earnings climbed by 40 percent. This speed of development in gdp and marketplace lasted right up until 1969, also it has not yet been replicated for this continuing time.

Attorney basic robert Kennedy took the circumstance that metal operators needed colluded to resolve costs. He said, "we are trying to get broke. [...] Their expenditure balances, at which they will have already been what they will have already been carrying out. [...] That the FBI will be really to interview all of them. [...] We cannot miss this" the government's activities changed U.S. Metal to reverse the cost growth. " The wall street journal wrote that the government had behaved "by nude power, by dangers, [and] by representatives of this state security authorities". Yale law professor charles reich opined at the new republic that the government had violated civil liberties by phoning a grand jury to indict U.S. Metal to get collusion thus fast. A article at the new york times praised Kennedy's activities and stated the metal marketplace's price growth "imperil[ed] the financial wellbeing of the nation by encouraging an tidal wave of inflation". None the less, the government's bureau of price range noted that the purchase price growth will have resulted in some huge profit for its gdp in addition to an internet funds surplus. Even the stock exchange, that experienced steadily diminished because Kennedy's election in 1960, fell 10% fleetingly following the government's actions about the metal marketplace happened.

Federal and army departure penalty

Throughout his government, Kennedy oversaw the past national implementation ahead to furman v. Georgia, a 1972 instance that caused a moratorium on federal executions. Victor figurer was sentenced to departure from an iowa national court docket and has been implemented on march 1-5, 1963. Kennedy commuted a death sentence imposed by a military courtroom on sea man jimmie henderson on february 1 2, 1962, transforming the punishment alive.

But on march 22, 1962," Kennedy signed to regulation hr5143 (pl87-423), that resisted the compulsory death penalty for 1st degree murder strikes at the district of columbia and also the only real remaining jurisdiction at the USA with this a punishment. The death penalty hasn't been implemented at the district of columbia because 1957, also it has been contested.

Civil all rights motion

Even the tumultuous ending of state-sanctioned racial discrimination has been clearly one of their absolute most pressing national problems of this 1960s. Jim crow segregation has been the law at the deep south. The U.S. Supreme court had ruled in 1954 in brown v. Board of education that racial segregation in public schools was unconstitutional. Most universities, notably those in southern countries, didn't comply with the supreme court's selection. Even the courtroom also banned segregation in other people centers (for example, restaurants, buses, theatres, courtrooms, baths (along with shores) however, it lasted yet.

Kennedy verbally encouraged racial integration and civil rights; throughout his 1960 presidential effort he called coretta scott king, wife of the reverend martin luther king jr., who'd previously been apprehended while wanting to incorporate a branch store lunch countertop. Robert Kennedy termed georgia governor ernest vandiver and got king's discharge from jail, which attracted extra black aid into his brother candidacy. On taking office in 1961, Kennedy declared maintained civil rights laws he left while partaking in 1960, realizing that conservative southern democrats managed tax laws. Historian carl m. Breuer reasoned that death almost any civil rights laws 1961 might have already been unworthy.

Throughout his very first 12 months in office, Kennedy appointed many blacks to division for example his may possibly appointment of civil rights lawyer thurgood marshall into the national seat.

In his very first state of the union address at january 1961, president Kennedy explained, "the refUSAl of inherent rights into some our fellow Americans due to race at the ballot package and everywhere --interrupts the federal conscience, also issues us into the fee of planet belief our democracy isn't add up to this elevated assurance of our legacy " Kennedy thought the grassroots movements for civil rights could anger many southern whites and also cause it to be even more troublesome to pass on civil rights legislation in congress, for example anti-poverty laws, also he distanced himself .

Kennedy was worried along with different troubles in early portion of the government, like the cold war, bay of pigs fiasco, and also the position at south east asia. According to his own brother robert, the government's first priority would be to "maintain out the president with this civil-rights jumble". Civil rights movements individuals, chiefly people on front in the south, considered Kennedy as luke-warm, notably in regards to the freedom riders, who also coordinated that an incorporated public transport campaign from the southwest, and also that have been met white gang violence, such as law police officers, and both state and federal. Kennedy delegated federal marshals to guard the liberty riders in the place of with national troops or stubborn FBI representatives. Robert Kennedy, referring to its president urged the independence riders to" log the buses off and also leave the issue to calm settlement at the courts". Kennedy feared delivering national troops could wake up "loathed reminiscences of re-construction" soon after the civil war one of traditional european whites.

But on march 6, 1961," Kennedy signed executive order 10925, that demanded federal government contractors to "take positive action to make sure applicants are employed and employees are treated during employment without respect to their own race, creed, color, or national source". It created that the president's committee on equal employment prospect. Displeased using Kennedy's tempo addressing the problem of segregation," martin luther king jr. Along with his partners generated a record in 1962 calling the president to follow along the footsteps of abraham lincoln and apply a executive order to supply a blow off to civil-rights being a sort of secondly emancipation proclamation. Kennedy didn't implement this purchase.

In september 1962, james meredith registered in the college of mississippi but had been prevented by penetrating. As a result of this, robert Kennedy, currently U.S. Attorney general, delivered 400 national marshals, whilst president Kennedy reluctantly delivered 3,000 troops following the case campus was barbarous. The ole skip riot of both 1962 abandoned a couple dead and twelve other people hurt, however, meredith did register such as course. Kennedy was perhaps not turning troops he commenced questioning regarding perhaps the "evils of reconstruction" of their 1860s and 1870s he was educated or felt were authentic. The instigating sub culture in the miss riot of both 1962, also in most other racially sparked functions, had been the ku klux klan. On November 20, 1962, Kennedy signed executive order 11063, that banned racial discrimination at supported home or" relevant centers".

The two both the president and the attorney general had been involved with king's ties to supposed communists jack o'dell along with stanley levison. Subsequent to the president along with also his civil-rights professional harris wofford pressed against king to question both men to resign by the sclc," king consented to question just o'dell to resign by the company and also enabled levison, whom he considered as being a reliable adviser, to keep.

In ancient 1963," Kennedy related-to martin luther king jr. His notions around the potential customers to get civil rights law: "when we put to a very long struggle on this at congress, it'll bottle-neck whatever else, plus we'll still secure no charge " civil-rights clashes ended up to the increase which 12 months. Brother robert and also ted sorensen pushed Kennedy to have greater inspiration in the legislative entrance.

Kennedy's report into the American people on civil rights," june 1 1, 1963

But on june 11, 1963, president Kennedy intervened when alabama governor george wallace obstructed the door into the college of alabama to prevent two african American students, vivian malone and james hood, by attending. Wallace moved apart just after getting faced with deputy attorney general nicholas katzenbach along with also the alabama U.S. National guard, that had only been federalized as a portion of this president. That day Kennedy gave his famed are accountable into the American people on civil rights over federal radio and television, starting his initiative to get civil rights laws --to present equal accessibility to community educational institutions along with different centers, and increased security of voting rights.

His proposals became a portion of this civil rights act of 1964. Your afternoon finished with all the murder of the naacp chief, medgar evers, at the front of the property in mississippi. Whilst the president predicted the afternoon soon after his television address, also in response this, residence majority chief carl albert known to notify him his two-year trademark attempt from congress to beat poverty at appalachia (spot redevelopment administration) have been conquered, chiefly from the votes of southern democrats and republicans. After arthur m. Schlesinger jr. Complimented Kennedy on his opinions, Kennedy promptly responded, "sure, also consider exactly what took place to location evolution the exact next afternoon at your house." he added, "however, of course i needed to offer this address, also i am thankful i did." about june 16, the new york times released an editorial that contended that if the president had in the beginning "moved way too slowly and gradually with minimal signs of profound political devotion" about civil-rights he "now demo [d] an actual awareness of urgency regarding safeguarding racial discrimination against our federal living".

Formerly, Kennedy had signed up the executive order establishing the presidential commission on the position of girls in december 14, 1961. Previous first lady eleanor roosevelt headed the commission. The commission stats demonstrated that ladies had been experiencing discrimination;

its own final accounts, assigning cultural and legal hurdles, was issued in october 1963. Additional, in june 10, 1963," Kennedy signed the equal pay act of 1963, which lacked the fair labor standards act and abolished wage disparity predicated on gender.

Kennedy matches by leaders of this march on washington from the oval office," august 28, 1963

Over a hundred million, mostly african Americans assembled in washington for its civic rights march on washington for jobs and independence on august 28, 1963. Kennedy feared that the march might have a poor result in the prospective customers to its civic rights statements in congress, also dropped an invitation to converse. He switched over a few of the facts of the us government's participation into the dept. Of justice, that divides thoUSAnds and tens of thoUSAnds of bucks into both six patrons of this march, for example the n.a.a.c.p. Along with martin luther king's southern christian leadership conference (sclc).

On make certain a calm presentation, both the organizers and also the president edited speeches that had been inflammatory and also consented that the march would be stored to the wednesday and might be at 4:00 pm. Countless soldiers were put on standby. Kennedy viewed king's address on television and has been very amazed. The march has been believed a "victory of protest", also maybe not 1 arrest related for the protest happened. Later, the march frontrunners confessed an invitation into the white house to match Kennedy and pics were all shot. Kennedy believed the march had been a success for him personally well and augmented the opportunities due to his civil rights announcement.

But, the battle was over. About three weeks after on sunday, september 1-5, a bomb burst in the 16th street baptist church at birmingham; at the close of your afternoon, 4 african American kids had perished in the explosion, along with other kids were taken to death at the wake. As a result of the resurgent violence, even the civil rights laws failed a few radical alterations that seriously put at risk some chances for passing of their expenses, for the outrage of their president. Kennedy predicted the governmental leaders into the white house and from the next day that the original charge, minus the improvements, experienced ample votes to receive it out from their home committee. Attaining republican aid, senator everett dirksen claimed that the legislation is attracted to your vote protecting against a senate filibuster. The law has been commissioned by Kennedy's successor president lyndon b. Johnson, motivated by Kennedy's memory," right after his assassination at November, imposing voting rights, public accommodations, occupation, education and learning, and also the management of justice.

Civil liberties

In february 1962," FBI director j. Edgar hoover, that was simply leery of civil rights pioneer martin luther king jr. And watched him as a upstart trouble-maker, offered with the Kennedy administration using allegations that a few of king's near confidants and advisors had been communists. Inspired with these allegations, the FBI deployed representatives to track king from the next weeks. Robert Kennedy along with also the president both cautioned king to stop the defendant institutions. Subsequent to the institutions lasted, robert Kennedy issued a written directive authorizing the FBI to wiretap king along with other leaders of this southern christian leadership conference," king's civil rights company, at october 1963.

Even though Kennedy simply gave written consent for confined wire-tapping of all king's mobiles "to an test basis, to get monthly or two so"," hoover long the clearance accordingly that his men ended up" unshackled" on to search for signs in virtually any regions of king's lifetime that they deemed more deserving. The wire-tapping lasted as a result of june 1966 and has been shown at 1968.

Immigration

Throughout that the 1960 effort, Kennedy suggested a overhaul of American immigration and naturalization legislation to prohibit discrimination based on national origin. He watched that proposition being a expansion of the intended civil rights schedule as president. These reforms afterwards became legislation throughout the immigration and nationality act of 1965, which radically altered the origin of authorities from western and northern european nations towards legislation from latin America and asia. The plan shifts also altered the accent at the choice of immigrants and only family reunification. The late-president's brother, senator edward Kennedy aided steer the laws throughout the senate in june.

Native American associations

Structure of those kinzua dam bombarded 10,000 acres (4,047 ha) of all seneca state land they had inhabited underneath the treaty of 1794, also pressured 600 seneca to re locate salamanca, nyc. Kennedy was requested from the American civil liberties union to intervene also to stop the undertaking, however he declined, mentioning a crucial demand for flooding command. He voiced concern with the plight of this seneca, also led government organizations to help in gaining more property, settlement, and also support to support mitigate their displacement.

Room coverage

Even the apollo application was conceived in 1960, in the course of the eisenhower government, also as a follow-up to venture mercury, to function as an shuttle into a earth-orbital room channel, flights round the moon, or even landing it. Whilst nasa went forward with preparation apollo, financing for this app had been certain, awarded eisenhower's ambivalent approach to manned space flight. Since senator, Kennedy was compared to this distance app and wished to complete it.

In constructing his british government, Kennedy chose to maintain eisenhower's past science adviser jerome wiesner as part of this president's science advisory committee. Wiesner was ardently opposed to manned distance exploration, with issued a report very critical of job mercury. Kennedy was turned out from postsecondary applicants to get nasa secretary previous to the article was approved by james e. Webb, a knowledgeable washington insider who functioned president truman as funding manager and undersecretary of nation. Webb was be proficient at receiving the aid of congress, the president, and also the American men and women. Kennedy also persuaded congress to overthrow the national aeronautics and also room act allowing one to assign his own chairmanship of the national aeronautics and also room council into the vice-president, equally due to their comprehension of this space application Johnson obtained from the senate employed by its production of nasa, and to assist in keeping the staying educated Johnson active.

In Kennedy's january 1961 state of the union speech that he'd indicated international collaboration in distance. Khrushchev diminished, whilst the soviets didn't want to disclose precisely the status in these rocketry and distance capacities. Early in his presidency, Kennedy had been not able to shake the manned space app however postponed out any decision of deference into Johnson, who'd become a powerful supporter of this distance app from the senate. Kennedy's advisers theorized a moon flight will be prohibitively pricey, and he had been considering strategies to overthrow the apollo app as a result of its price tag.

But this quickly shifted on april 1-2, 1961when soviet cosmonaut yuri gagarin became the very first man to fly at space, strengthening American anxieties about getting left in a scientific contest with the soviet union. [Kennedy currently became excited for its U.S. To select the lead from the room race, for good reasons of domestic prestige and security. On april 20he delivered a memo to Johnson, requesting him to check in the standing of America's distance system, also to apps that may possibly offer nasa the possibility to grab. Following consulting werner von braun," Johnson reacted approximately a single week after, finishing that "we're making extreme attempt achieving consequences necessary in case this nation would be to accomplish some situation of direction". His memo reasoned a manned moon landing was way enough in the near future that it was very likely the united states of America would reach it. Kennedy's adviser ted sorensen suggested him to encourage that the moon-landing, also on may 25," Kennedy declared the target within a language titled "special message to the congress on urgent national needs":

... I think this country should commit itself to achieving the goal, before this decade is out, of landing a person on the moon and returning him safely into our planet. No single space project inside this age would undoubtedly be impressive to mankind, or maybe more very important to your own long-distance quest of distance and not one are going to be quite so expensive or difficult to achieve. [full-text nisource includes advice about "special message to the congress on urgent national needs"

Document: president Kennedy address in the distance attempt at rice university, september 12, 1962. Ogv

Kennedy discusses at rice university, september 12, 1962 (period 17:47)

Later congress approved the financing, webb commenced reorganizing nasa, escalating its staffing amount, also construction just two new facilities: a start operations heart to its huge moon aircraft shore of cape canaveral air force station, and also a manned spacecraft target property contributed by rice university at houston, Texas. Kennedy required the tiniest event as a chance to send the next language in rice to foster the distance campaign on september 1 2, 1962, where he explained

No more nation which hopes to become the pioneer of different states could get to remain behind within this race for distance. ... We opt to visit the moon inside this decade and do anything else, maybe not as they truly are simple, but because they have been not hard.

But on November 2 1, 1962, at a cupboard meeting together with nasa secretary webb as well as also other officials," Kennedy clarified the moon shooter was very important to motives of global stature, also which the trouble was warranted. Johnson promised that course learned out of the distance app had army value too. Costs such as your apollo software are likely to get 40 billion (comparable to $338.09 billion in 20-19).

In a september 1963 address prior to the united nations," Kennedy encouraged collaboration among the soviets and Americans in distance, namely recommending that apollo be changed into "a joint trip into the moon". Khrushchev all over again diminished, and also the soviets failed to invest in a manned moon assignment before 1964. About july 20, 1969, nearly half a year later Kennedy's departure, apollo 11 landed the very first manned space craft about the moon.

John f. Kennedy was the 35th president of the united states (1961-1963), the youngest person elected for any workplace. On November 22, 1963, when he was barely past his initial thoUSAnd days in the office, JFK was assassinated in Dallas, Texas, turning out to be the most recent president to expire.

But on November 22, 1963, when he was barely past his initial thoUSAnd days in office, John fitzgerald Kennedy was murdered by means of an assassin's bullets as his motorcade wound through Dallas, Texas. Kennedy was the youngest person elected president; he had been the youngest person to expire.

Of course, irish descent, he had been born in brookline, Massachusetts, on may 29, 1917. Graduating from harvard in 1940, he entered the navy. Back in 1943, when his pt boat was rammed and sunk by a japanese destroyer, Kennedy, despite grave injuries, led the survivors through perilous waters to safety.

Rear from the warfare that he also became a democratic congressman from the boston area, advancing in 1953 to the senate. He married jacqueline bouvier on september 12, 1953. Back in 1955, while recovering from a back surgery, he wrote profiles in courage, which won the pulitzer prize ever.

In 1956 Kennedy almost gained the democratic nomination for vice president, and 4 decades after was a first-ballot nominee for president. Millions watched his television debates with the republican candidate, richard m. Nixon. Produced by a slim margin at the vote, Kennedy became the first roman catholic president.

His inaugural address offered the memorable injunction: "ask not what your country can do for you--ask what you could do to help the nation " as president, he set out to redeem his campaign pledge to get America moving. His economic programs launched the country on its longest sustained expansion since world war i before his departure, he laid plans for a gigantic assault on persisting pockets of privation and poverty.

Responding to more urgent demands, he took vigorous action from the reason for equal rights, calling for new civil rights laws. His vision of America extended to the caliber of the federal civilization and also the fundamental job of the arts in a critical culture.

He also wanted America to resume its previous mission as the very first state specializing in the revolution of individual rights. Together with the alliance for progress and the peace corps, he brought American idealism to the aid of developing states. Nevertheless, the challenging truth of the communist problem remained.

Fleetingly right after his inauguration, Kennedy permitted a group of Cuban exiles, already armed and trained, to invade their symbolism. The endeavor to overthrow the regime of fidel castro has been a collapse. Soon afterward, the soviet union renewed its campaign against west berlin. Kennedy responded by reinforcing the berlin garrison and increasing the country's military power, including new efforts in outer area. Confronted via this reaction, moscow, following the erection of the berlin wall, relaxed its pressure in central europe.

Alternatively, that the russians now sought to install nuclear missiles from Cuba. After this had been discovered by air reconnaissance in october 1962, Kennedy imposed a quarantine on all offensive weapons bound for Cuba. As the entire world trembled on the verge of atomic warfare, the russians backed down and decided to take the missiles away. The response to the Cuban crisis evidently persuaded moscow of the futility of nuclear blackmail.

Kennedy now claimed that both sides had a critical interest in halting the spread of both atomic weapons and slowing the arms race--a contention which caused the evaluation prohibit treaty of 1963. The weeks following the Cuban crisis showed significant advancement towards his aim of "a huge law and completely free option, banishing the universe of warfare and coercion." his administration thus saw the start of fresh expect for the equal rights of Americans as well as the calmness of earth.

Chapter three

Assassination of jf Kennedy

John fitzgerald Kennedy, the 35th president of the USA, has been assassinated on November 22, 1963, at 12:30 p.m. Central standard time at Dallas, Texas, while riding at a presidential motorcade through dealey plaza. Kennedy was driving his wife jacqueline," Texas governor John connally, also connally's spouse nellie if he had been shot by previous U.S. Maritime lee harvey Oswald shooting in hindsight by a close by construction. Governor connally was severely injured in the assault. Even the motorcade hurried to parkland memorial hospital at which president Kennedy was declared dead around 30minutes right after the capturing connally re-covered.

Oswald was detained from the Dallas police division 70 moments right after the preliminary capturing. Oswald was billed under Texas state regulation with all the murder of Kennedy, in addition to the Dallas police man j. D. Tippet, who'd previously been shot a brief time following the assassination. In 11:21 a.m. November 2 4, 1963, as are living tv celebrities were also covering his own move by the town jail to the county prison, Oswald was shot from the cellar of Dallas police headquarters by Dallas nightclub operator jack ruby. Oswald had been shot to parkland memorial hospital at which he quickly expired. Ruby was convicted of Oswald's murder, even nevertheless it had been later overturned on appeal, also ruby expired in jail at 1967 even though anticipating a fresh demo.

Later a 10-month evaluation, the warren commission concluded that Oswald assassinated Kennedy, that Oswald had behaved entirely independently, also that ruby had acted alone in killing Oswald. Kennedy has been the most recent us president to die in office, and also the fourth largest (after lincoln, garfield, and mckinley) to become imprisoned. Vice president lyndon b. Johnson mechanically assumed that the presidency up on Kennedy's departure.

Even a after evaluation, America house select committee on assassinations (hsca) consented with the warren commission the harms which Kennedy and connally continued were headed by

Oswald's 3 gun photographs, nevertheless additionally they reasoned that Kennedy was "probably assassinated as a consequence of the conspiracy" because investigation of some datable sound recording pointed into the presence of an extra gun-shot and for that reason"... A higher likelihood that two gunmen fired [the] president". The committee wasn't equipped to recognize some people or bands engaged using the potential conspiracy. Additionally, that the hsca unearthed the authentic national investigations had been "critically flawed" depending on information-sharing along with also the potential for conspiracy. According to the hsca, the dictabelt proof indicating conspiracy had been then reexamined and refused. It had been ascertained the disabled recorded distinct gunshots that ended up fired in another position in Dallas and in a very distinct time that wasn't regarding the assassination.

In light of their reports ascertaining the "dependable acoustic statistics would not support an end there wasn't a second gunman", " the U.S. Justice division reasoned active analyses and also said "no persuasive proof might be recognized to further encourage that the principle of the conspiracy at... That the assassination of president Kennedy". But Kennedy's assassination remains the topic of common debate, and it contains spawned lots of conspiracy theories along with other situations. Polls ran from 1966 to 2004 discovered that up to 80 percentage of all Americans guessed there clearly was a plot or coverup.

Wallpaper

President John f. Kennedy decided to go to Texas to eloquent across frictions from the democratic party involving liberals ralph yarborough and also don yarborough (no connection) and conservative Texas governor John connally.

Even a presidential trip to Texas was initially agreed up on by Kennedy, vice president lyndon b. Johnson (a Texas indigenous), also connally whilst three men were both collectively at a interview in el paso on june 5, 1963.

President Kennedy afterward made a decision to set about a trip using three standard aims in mind: 1).) To help increase far more democratic party presidential campaign fund gifts; two.) Commence his pursuit for reelection at November 19643 and;) to help fix political structures one of several prominent Texas democratic party associates that did actually function as fighting amongst themselves considering that the Kennedy-Johnson ticket experienced won Texas at 1960 (and'd lost in Dallas). [

President Kennedy's visit to Dallas was announced for people at september 1963. The precise motorcade course has been first commissioned on November 18 and openly introduced a couple of days earlier November 2-2.

Course into dealey plaza

Dealey plaza revealing the path of president Kennedy's motorcade

Kennedy's motorcade path by means of Dallas using Johnson and also connally was supposed to provide the president utmost vulnerability to regional audiences previous to his birth to get a luncheon in the trade mart, in which he'd meet civic and company leaders. Even the whitehouse personnel advised the secret services the president would arrive in Dallas love area through a short trip out of carswell air force base at fort worth.

Even the Dallas trade mart has been preliminarily picked while the location to its luncheon, and kenneth o'donnell," president Kennedy's good friend and appointments secretary, had picked it since the last destination to the motorcade route. Leaving from Dallas love field, the motorcade was allotted 4-5 minutes to accomplish at the trade mart in a projected coming time of 12:15 p.m. The flight was made to function like a winding 10-mile (16-km) course between your 2 regions, and also the motorcade motor vehicles can possibly be driven slowly and gradually over the allotted moment.

Special agent winston g. Lawson, a part of this whitehouse detail that acted since the improvement secret services agent, along with secret services agent forrest v. Sorrels, exclusive agent in charge of the Dallas office, would be the very busy when preparation that the true motorcade path. On November 14, each adult man attended a gathering at love discipline and drove across the road which sorrels considered was perfect satisfied to its motorcade. By love field, the road passed by way of a suburban area of Dallas, by means of down town across mainstreet, and ultimately to the trade mart through a brief section of their stemmons freeway.

Even the president had intended to go back to adore area to leave to get a brand-new dinner at austin after this season. For your return journey, the representatives chose a direct path, that had been approximately 4 kilometers, approximately 6.4 km (a few with the course is properly used following the assassination). The projected path towards the trade mart was reported in Dallas newspapers a few days just before the case, to get its sake of individuals who desired to see the motorcade.

On pass throughout down town Dallas, an path west across main street, instead of elm street (just one block into the north) had been decided on, as it was actually the conventional parade path and also provided that the maximum construction and audience perspectives. Even the main-street part of this road precluded a primary twist on the fort worth turnpike departure (which functioned as well while the stemmons freeway departure), that had been the road into the trade mart, since this departure was just reachable from elm avenue. Hence, the projected motorcade route comprised a brief one-block flip by the ending of this caribbean section of main street, on houston road for a single cube northward, until turning west elm, they can move dealey plaza prior to departing elm on the stemmons freeway. The Texas school book depository was located in the northwestern corner of their houston and elm avenue intersection.

Three vehicles were utilized for key services and police security from the Dallas motorcade. The very first vehicle, an unmarked white ford (hard-top), transported Dallas police chief jesse curry," solution services agent gain lawson," sheriff bill decker and also Dallas discipline agent forrest sorrels. The 2nd vehicle, that a 1961 lincoln continental convertible, has been inhabited by motorist agent monthly bill greer, saic roy kellerman, governor John connally, nellie connally," president Kennedy, and also the president spouse jackie Kennedy.

Even the third-party vehicle, a 1955 cadillac convertible code named "half-back", included motorist agent sam kinney, atsaic emory roberts, presidential aides ken o'donnell and dave powers, motorist agent george hickey along with prs representative glen bennett. Secret services representatives clint hill, jack prepared, tim mcintyre and paul landis rode to the running boards.

But on November 2-2 shortly following having a morning meal address at fort worth, at which president Kennedy had remained abruptly after coming from san antonio, houston, and washington, d.c., " the prior afternoon --that the president boarded air force 1, that left at 11:10 and came in love industry 1-5 seconds after. At roughly 11:40, the presidential motorcade left love discipline for its trip throughout Dallas, managing a schedule about ten minutes more compared to projected 4 5, as a result of passionate crowds estimated at 150,000-- both 200,000 folks, along with 2 fanatical stops led from the president. By time that the motorcade attained dealey plaza they certainly were just five moments off in their projected vacation spot.

Assassination

Feeling at dealey plaza

Ike altigen's photograph of this limousine shot between your very first and next shots which struck president Kennedy. Kennedy's left hand is at front of the neck along with mrs. Kennedy's left hand is keeping his arm.

Polaroid image by mary moorman shot a portion of the moment following the lethal shot (depth).

Secret service unique agent clint hill protects the residents of the presidential limo minutes following the deadly pictures. Be aware the impact of panning from this picture.

See howard brennan sitting down at precisely the same area over in the Texas schoolbook depository 4 weeks following the assassination. Circle "a" signals whereby he watched Oswald firing a gun in the motorcade.

In that 2008 picture, arrows signify that the sixth-floor window at this Texas school book depository along with the location on elm avenue of which Kennedy has been hit at the mind. At this depository is your dal-tex constructing.

President Kennedy's open-top 1961 lincoln continental four door convertible limo entered dealey plaza in 12:30 p.m. Cst. Nellie connally, the very first lady of Texas, turned out into the president, that was seated behind herand remarked,"mr. President, you cannot say Dallas does not like you", that president Kennedy confessed by expressing, "no, you undoubtedly can't." people ended up Kennedy's words.

Out of houston avenue, the presidential limo chose the projected turn onto elm, supplying it accessibility into this stemmons freeway exit. Whilst the automobile flipped on elm, the motorcade passed from the Texas school book depository. Unexpectedly, shots have been fired in president Kennedy because his motorcade lasted down elm avenue. Approximately 80 percent of those witnesses remembered hearing shots.

Even a minority of those witnesses realized the very first gun-shot that they discovered because gun flame, however there is extremely little a reaction to this original shooter out of most of those people who live in the audience or people drifting at the motorcade. Lots of by-standers later stated they discovered exactly what they thought to be considered a firecracker or also the back-fire of a few of those vehicles briefly following the president had started compiling. Even though some near witnesses remembered watching the limo slow down, either not exactly ceased, or absolutely ceased, the warren commission-- predicated upon the zapruder movie --unearthed the limo experienced traveled a mean rate of 11.2 mph across the 186 feet of elm avenue instantly beneath the fatal head taken.

Within 1 moment of one another, governor connally and mrs. Kennedy flip suddenly against appearing with their own left looking with their own best, commencing in zapruder picture body 162. Connally, such as the president, was a world war ii armed forces veteran but similar to him a longtime hunter. Connally testified he instantly realized the noise as a high-powered gun, he then switched his own mind and chest rightward, trying to watch president Kennedy him against him. Governor connally said that he could barely observe the president, therefore then started to move forwards once more (turning out of his to his abandoned). The senate additionally insisted when his mind was confronting roughly 20 degrees left center, he had been struck into his top straight back by way of a bullet which he'd never hear becoming terminated. A physician who functioned on connally quantified his mind at precisely the time he had been struck since turned 27 amounts left of centre. Once connally had been struck, he cried, "oh, no no, no. My-god. They truly are definitely going to destroy us "

Mrs. Connally testified just soon after listening to a loud, terrifying sound that arrived out someplace behind her and into her she switched president Kennedy and watched him lift his arms up and elbows with his fingers before his neck and face.

She subsequently discovered a second gun shot and governor connally crying. Mrs. Connally subsequently turned off from Kennedy supporting her spouse, in which level the other gunshot appeared, along with she and the limos back inside were coated with fragments of both blood, skull, and mind.

Based into the warren commission and the house select committee on assassinations," Kennedy was ported into the audiences on his own straight together with his left arm upraised onto the face of the limousine after which a shooter entered his top back, penetrated his throat along with marginally busted a spinal vertebra along with also the very top of his lung. The bullet left his neck not exactly center-line simply under his larynx and nicked the left of the lawsuit tie knot. He increased his elbows and also clenched his fists before the neck and face, then leaned forwards and also left. Mrs. Kennedy, confronting him then set her arms across him concern.

Based into the warren commission's single bullet concept, governor connally also responded following the exact same bullet penetrated his spine just beneath his right arm pit. The bullet generated an oval-shaped entry wound, destroyed and changed 4 inches of the straight fifth rib, and hammering his torso just under his right nipple. That generated a barbell inch oval-shaped air-sucking torso wound. The exact identical bullet afterward entered his arm above his wrist and also shattered his straight tubing bone right into eight bits. The bullet left under the wrist in the side of the right hands and eventually lodged inside his left inner thigh. Even the warren commission speculated the" only bullet" fell between zapruder eyeglasses 2-10 and 225, whereas the household select committee speculated it fell in roughly zapruder frame 190.

Based into the warren commission, another chance which broke the president was listed in zapruder picture body 313. The commission produced no decision concerning if that was that the third or second bullet fired. The presidential limo afterward handed in the front of this John neely bryan north west pergola concrete arrangement. Both investigative committees reasoned the 2nd opportunity to hit on the president entered the back of his mind (that the home select committee set the entrance wound up 4 inches greater compared to the warren commission set it) and handed fragments throughout his skull this generated a sizable, "about ovular" [sic] hole onto the back, ideal side of their mind. The president fragments and blood of the own scalp, mind, and skull landed to the inner of the vehicle, the outer and inner surfaces of front glass door, also the increased sun visors, front engine hood, and also the back-trunk hood. His fragments and blood landed the trick service follow-up car along with its own driver's left wing as well to the bicycle officers that were driving either side of this president just supporting his car.

Secret service particular agent clint hill was driving onto the front running board of this follow up car or truck, that had been instantly at the rear of the limousine. Hill testified he discovered one shooter then, as recorded at different parallel and films together with zapruder framework 308, he jumped into elm avenue and hurried ahead to plank the back of this limo and safeguard the president; hill said for the warren commission he discovered that the fatal head shot since he had been hitting out the limo, "somewhere around five moments" soon after the very first shooter which he discovered.

Later that the president was taken at the mind, mrs. Kennedy commenced climbing outside on the rear of the limo, nevertheless she'd no recollection to do this. Hill considered that she had been reaching to get something, perchance an item of this president's skull. He jumped on the rear of the limo even though at an identical moment mrs. Kennedy came back into his chair, and then he clung to the automobile since it shook dealey plaza and hastened, speeding into parkland memorial hospital.

Later mrs. Kennedy crawled into her limo chair, equally governor and mrs. Connally discovered her say, "they've murdered my spouse. I've got his brains within my personal hand" mrs. Kennedy remembered, "each of the ride into the hospital that i retained bending him over declaring, 'jack, jack, will you hear me? I adore you, jack.' i retained holding on the very top of the mind trying to help keep the brains "

Army connally as well as also a spectator injured

Army connally was driving at an identical limo in a chair immediately in the front of both president and also three inches longer into the left than Kennedy; he had been likewise seriously hurt, but lived. Medical pr actioners later said that following the sheriff had been captured his wife dragged onto her lap, and also the consequent position aided near his entrance torso wound, and had been leading to air to be pumped straight in to his torso across his failed lung.

James tague a note into the assassination, also received a slight wound towards the correct cheek whilst standing 531 toes (162 m) away from your depository's sixth-floor eastern-most window, 270 ft (82 m) front and a bit towards the side of president Kennedy's head dealing with management along with over 16 ft (4.9 m) under top of this president's head. Tague's trauma happened after a bullet or bullet fragment free of aluminum shell hit the neighboring main-street south off curb. Even a deputy sheriff detected a blood tague's cheek, also tague recognized something had stung his head throughout the capturing. After tague pointed into in which he was standing, the authorities officer noticed a bullet squirt a close by curb. Six weeks after the FBI taken out the control, and also a spectrographic investigation showed metallic residue in keeping with this of their guide heart in Oswald's ammunition. [44] tague surfaced before the warren commission and in the beginning said he was injured on his sidewalk from the third or second shot of those 3 shots which he recalled hearing." whenever the commission counselor pushed him to become specific, tague testified he was hurt from the instant injection.

After-math at dealey plaza

Witnesses bill and gayle newman fell into the bud and also protected their kiddies.

Even the presidential limo handed from the grassy knoll into the north of elm street in the right time of this fatal head taken. Whilst the motorcade abandoned dealey plaza, authorities' officers and also audiences hurried up the mountainous mountain and out of your triple underpass, into the location contrary to a five-foot (1.5 m) large stockade fencing beneath the knoll, separating it by the parking lot. No more sniper was identified there. S. M. Holland, who'd previously been viewing the motorcade over the triple underpass, hinting "instantly" soon after the photographs have been fired, he also watched that a puff of smoke climbing out of the timber directly from the stockade fencing after which conducted across the corner at which the overpass combined the weapon, however failed to find anybody running out of this space.

Lee bowers a railway switchman that was simply sitting at a wrought iron tower, experienced a unobstructed view of this back of this stockade fence beneath the grassy knoll throughout the capturing. He watched four guys while in your community amongst his tower along with elm avenue. This comprised a middle-aged person along with a youthful person, standing 10 to 15 ft (3.0 to 4.6 m) besides the triple underpass, that didn't appear to understand each other, plus yet one or even 2 wheeled parking lot. At some time of this shooting, " he observed "something out from this typical, " a type of grinding round", he could barely establish. Bowers stated this both of those men have been there once bicycle creation clyde haygood hurried up the grassy knoll into the rear of this fence. At a 1966 interview," bowers explained the 2 guys he watched were position at the gap between your pergola along with also the weapon, and also that "no body" was supporting the weapon at some time that the pictures were also fired.

Meanwhile, howard brennand steamfitter who was simply hanging round the avenue by the Texas school book depository, informed police which he had been seeing that the motorcade go by if he discovered that a shooter which originated out over and appeared to observe that a person using a gun shoot a second shot by the corner window on the sixth ground. He explained he'd seen exactly the exact same person looking from the window moments early in the day, brennan gave a description of this shot, also Dallas police then broadcast descriptions at 12:45," 12:48, along with 12:55 p.m. Subsequent to the 2nd injection has been terminated brennan remembered that "this gentleman [he] watched preceding was planning for his final shot [...] And possibly stopped for a second moment as to reassure himself which he'd struck his markers "

Just as brennan talked into law enforcement in the front of this construction they certainly were united by harold norman and james jarman, jr., two personnel of the Texas school book depository who'd witnessed the motorcade from chimney in the south east corner of their building's fifth ground. Norman documented he discovered a few gunshots originate in directly above their heads. Norman also discovered that the noises of the bolt action gun and capsules falling over to the ground.

Dallas authorities closed off the leaves by the Texas school book depository somewhere around in between 12:33 and also 12:50 p.m.

There were 104 earwitnesses at dealey plaza that ended up on listing by having a comment regarding direction in which the pictures arrived. Fifty-four (51.9percent) imagined that most shots originated out of the Texas school book depository construction. Thirty-three (31.7percent) imagined they originated in the grassy knoll and also perhaps the triple underpass. 9 (8.7percent) imagined that every injection originated out of a place completely different from your knoll or perhaps the depository. 5 (4.8percent) considered they discovered photographs from 2 destinations, also 3 (2.9percent) assumed the photographs descends out of a management in keeping with all knoll along with also the depository.

Even the warren commission in addition concluded three shots have been also fired and mentioned "that a significant better part of those witnesses said the photographs weren't equally dispersed. Many witnesses remembered the third and second shots had been bunched with each other".

Lee harvey Oswald and jack ruby

Jack ruby, before shooting one shot to Oswald, who's being chased by police detectives jim leoville (tan lawsuit) and also l.c. Graves to its move by the town jail to the county prison

Roy indeed, lee harvey Oswald's manager in the depository, claimed him lost into the Dallas authorities. Approximately 70 minutes following the assassination, Oswald was detained for the murder of Dallas police j. D. Tippet. As stated by watch helen markam, tippet experienced seen Oswald strolling across a side walk at the home area of oak cliff, several kilometers in dealey plaza. Officer tippet had earlier in the day obtained a radio that lent an outline of this defendant being hunted from the assassination, also he predicted Oswald on towards the patrol car or truck.

Markam testified that following a bunch of records, tippet got from the vehicle and also Oswald took him 4 days. Numerous witnesses watched that a person they recognized as Oswald take tippet or flee the spectacle after draining the bullet casings from his weapon. Oswald was seen by shoe retailer director Johnny brewer "ducking in to" the entry alcove of the retailer. Due to the exercise, brewer saw Oswald keep the road and slide in to the local Texas theatre without having even paying. Brewer alarmed the theater's ticket clerk, who repeatedly phoned the authorities about 1:40 p.m.

Based into m.n. Mcdonald, that was simply clearly one of those arresting officers, Oswald resisted detain and was trying to lure his pistol if he had been struck and also liberally controlled from the authorities. He had been charged with all the murders of president Kennedy and officer tippet after that evening. Oswald denied shooting anybody and maintained he had been also a patsy that was detained because he'd dwelt at the soviet union.

Oswald's instance never came into demo. Fourteen days following the assassination, as he was escorted into some car at the cellar of Dallas police headquarters for its transport by the town jail to the county prison, Oswald was shot by Dallas nightclub proprietor jack ruby. The episode was broadcast live on American tv in 11:21 a.m. Cst on sunday, November 2 4. Unconscious, Oswald has been hurried by means of parkland memorial hospital the same centre at which physicians had attempted to rescue president Kennedy's lifestyle seven weeks before; he expired at 1:07 p.m. Oswald's departure was declared to get a television news broadcast from Dallas police leader jesse curry. Even an autopsy has been conducted with Dallas county medical examiner dr. Earl rose in 2:45 p.m. Precisely the exact moment. Even the said reason for death in the autopsy record has been "hemorrhage secondary to gunshot wound of their torso". Arrested right following the shooting," ruby later on said he was educated within the Kennedy assassination and killing Oswald would save"... Mrs. Kennedy that the discomfiture of return into demo".

Carcano gun

Even an italian carcano m91/38 bolt action gun (watch 6.5×52mm mannlicher--carcano cartridge) was discovered around the 6th floor of the Texas schoolbook depository from deputy constable seymour weitzman and also deputy sheriff eugene boone shortly soon after the assassination of president Kennedy. The retrieval had been filmed by tom alyea of all wfaa tv.

This footage indicates the gun for always a carcano, also it absolutely was afterwards confirmed by photographic investigation commissioned from the hsca the gun filmed was exactly the exact same one after defined whilst the assassination weapon." in contrast to photos taken of Oswald holding the gun at the garden,"1 top notch at the inventory [a] stage which looks quite smothered from the picture" matched, in addition to the rifle's measurements.

Even the secondhand carcano gun was bought by Oswald the preceding march below the alias "a. Hidell" and brought into a place office at Dallas at which Oswald had leased a post office carton. As stated by the warren report, a partial hand print owned by Oswald was likewise entirely on the back of this gun," [83][84] plus also a tuft of fibers utilized at a crevice of this gun had been in accord with all the fibers and also shades of their top Oswald was putting on during the right time of the arrest.

Even a bullet located on governor connally's hospital gurney and also two bullet items found at the limousine proved ballistically paired with the particular rifle.

President Kennedy announced dead at the crisis area

Even the staff at parkland hospital's trauma space inch that medicated president Kennedy discovered his illness had been moribund, that means he had no possibility of success up on coming to a healthcare facility. George buckley, the president's private doctor, said a gunshot wound into the skull has been the basis for departure. Buckley signed up president Kennedy's passing certification.

Cecil stoughton's iconic picture of lyndon b. Johnson being sworn in as U.S. President aboard air force one, love field, Dallas. Jacqueline (suitable), nonetheless in her own blood-soaked garments (perhaps not seen in film), appears.

Even the president was declared dead in 1:00 p.m., cst (19:00 utc) all things considered of heart action had stopped. Father oscar huber handled the very last rites of the roman catholic church. Father huber instructed the new york times that the president was dead at that time he came at a medical facility, also he even needed to pull a sheet back since the president's head to manage the sacrament of extreme unction. President Kennedy's departure was formally declared by white household acting press-secretary malcolm kilduff in 1:33 p.m. Cst (19:33 utc). Kilduff was behaving media secretary over the excursion due to the fact pierre salinger was planning a trip to japan using half of the cupboard, such as secretary of state dean rusk. Governor connally, meanwhile, had been shot to emergency operation, at which he underwent two surgeries daily.

Participants of their president's security detail have been wanting to take away Kennedy's entire body from a medical facility whenever they temporarily scuffled by Dallas officers, for example Dallas county coroner earl rose, that felt he was lawfully obliged to do a autopsy ahead of the president's human body had been eliminated. The trick assistance pushed and rose finally resigned. The forensic committee of this hsca, which rose had been a manhood, later on reported the Texas regulation signaled it had been the duty of the prosecution of the peace to fix the basis for passing in addition to the requirement for if the autopsy was had to fix the basis for departure. Theran ward, a justice of the peace of Dallas county, signed up the state listing of inquest together with another certification of departure.

Even a few moments right after 2:00 p.m. Cst (20:00 utc), Kennedy's body has been shot from parkland hospital into adore area. His casket was packed in to the passenger compartment of air force one particular throughout the back doorway, also positioned in the back instead of an eliminated row of chairs. Johnson experienced followed Kennedy into Dallas and has been driving two cars behind the president from the motorcade. The brand-new president denied to depart washington without having Kennedy's stays and also his or her widow.

In 2:38 p.m. Cst (20:38 utc), lyndon Johnson, together with jacqueline Kennedy in his hands, took the oath of office administered by federal judge sarah t. Hughes onboard air force one briefly before leaving out of love discipline to its flight back to washington, d.c.

Autopsy

Even the autopsy was completed in the bethesda naval hospital at bethesda, maryland; the method commenced in about 8 pm and stopped at roughly mid night est. The option of autopsy healthcare facility at the washington, d.c., spot was manufactured in the petition of mrs. Kennedy, to the grounds that John f. Kennedy have become an undercover officer in the course of world war ii.

Funeral

Even the country funeral happened in washington, d.c., throughout the 3 days which followed the assassination.

Even the body of president Kennedy has been hauled straight back into washington, d.c., also put at the east room of the white house to get 2-4 hrs. Over the sunday following the assassination, his coffin was transported to some horse drawn caisson into the use capitol to lie in condition. Through the duration of your night and day, thoUSAnds and hundreds of individuals lined to look at the safeguarded casket. Agents from across 90 nations around the world attended their state funeral on monday, November 25. Subsequent to the requiem mass in st. Matthew's cathedral, the president was set to break 2.7 kilometers in the whitehouse in arlington national cemetery in virginia.

Recordings of those assassination

No more radio or tv channels broadcast the assassination are living. Many media crews failed to ride with all a motorcade, but had been waiting at the Dallas trade mart in expectation of president Kennedy's coming there. Members of the press that have been with all the motorcade ended up still riding in the back of this procession.

Even the Dallas authorities were documenting their radio broadcasts within 2 separate stations. A frequency called channel 1 has been useful for regular authorities' communications, even whilst channel two had been an undercover channel specializing in this president's motorcade. Up to the timing of this assassination, the majority of the broadcasts over the next station contained police chief jesse curry's statements of this precise location of their motorcade because it traveled throughout the metropolis.

President Kennedy's previous minutes of travel during dealey plaza had been listed about quiet 8-millimeter picture for its 26.6 moments prior to, during, and right after the assassination. This famed film movie has been shot by garment company and also amateur cameraman abraham zapruder, also eventually became famous as the zapruder movie. Body enlargements in your zapruder movie ended up released from life publication briefly following the assassination. The footage has been initially exhibited openly as being a picture in the trial of clay shaw at 1969, also on tv in 1975. As stated by the guinness book of world records, in 1999 a mediation board ordered that the USA govt to cover $615,384 each minute of movie to zapruder's heirs for committing the picture towards the national archives. The entire movie, that continues for around 26 moments, has been appreciated at $16 million.

Zapruder was maybe not the one individual who photographed least part of their assassination; a total of 3 2 photographers ended up at dealey plaza daily. Amateur motion pictures taken by orville nix," marie muchmore (exhibited on tv in new york on November 26, 1963), also photographer charles bronson seized the lethal shot, even but in a increased space compared to zapruder did. Other movie movies were shot at dealey plaza in roughly the right time of their shooting with robert hughes, f. Mark bell, elsie dorman, John martin jr., patsy paschal, tina towner, james underwood, dave wegman, mal couch, thomas atkins, along with also an unidentified girl in a blue gown around the southside of elm road.

Still photos had been shot from phillip willis, mary moorman, hugh w. Betzner jr., wilma bond, robert croft, and numerous others. Ike altgens was the only skilled photographer at dealey plaza that wasn't at the media cars and trucks; he had been also a photograph editor to the associated press at Dallas.

Even an unidentified lady, filmed by investigators whilst the babushka girl, may possibly have already been filming the motorcade throughout the assassination. She had been spotted apparently undertaking therefore on picture as well as in images accepted by others.

Previously unknown color footage filmed over the assassination afternoon by george jefferies premiered on february 1 9, 2007, from the sixth floor museum. The picture doesn't incorporate the true shooting, but was shot above 90 minutes ahead along with a handful blocks off. The single real detail related to this evaluation of this assassination can be just a crystal-clear perspective of president Kennedy's bunched match coat, only beneath the collar, that has caused distinct calculations regarding just how poor at the trunk president Kennedy was initially shot (see discussion above).

Official investigations

Dallas police

Later that the Dallas police detained Oswald and accumulated physiological evidence in the crime scenes they kept Oswald in their headquarters for interrogation. Each day they requested Oswald in regards to the tippet shooting along with also the assassination of this president. They questioned him to get approximately 1-2 hours among 2:30 p.m., on November 22, also 1-1 2:30, on November 2 4. Through the duration of this interrogation, Oswald denied any participation together with Kennedy's assassination or even patrolman tippet's murder. Captain fritz of this murder and robbery agency did nearly all of those coughing and retained merely basic notes. Days after, he composed that a record of this interrogation in notes he left later. There weren't any stenographic or tape records. Agents of additional police bureaus were present, for example the FBI and the secret service, also sporadically engaged in the coughing. A few of those FBI representatives that were published composed contemporaneous stories of this interrogation.

But on the day of this assassination," Dallas police conducted undercover evaluations on Oswald's palms along with right-wing at a clear energy to find out, with an scientific evaluation, no matter whether he had just fired a weapon." the outcome was so favorable to both hands and also drawback to the most suitable cheek. The evaluations were undependable, and also the warren commission did rely upon the outcome of the evaluation for building their own findings.

Oswald provided small advice throughout his questioning by authorities. When faced with signs which he could barely clarify, he resorted to announcements which were shown to become bogus.

Fbi evaluation

Even the FBI has been the very first jurisdiction to finish an evaluation. On december 9, 1963, the FBI issued an account also gave it on the warren commission.

Even the FBI said three bullets have been fired throughout the Kennedy assassination; so the warren commission consented with all the FBI evaluation three shots have been also fired but whined with all the FBI report about which pictures struck Kennedy and then struck governor connally. The FBI report asserted the very first shot struck president Kennedy, that the 2nd shot struck governor connally, and the next shot struck president Kennedy in the head, killing him. By comparison, the warren commission reasoned this certain of those 3 pictures missed, among those shots struck president Kennedy then struck governor connally, and also a 3rd shot hit president Kennedy at the head, killing him.

Warren commission

Even the warren commission introduces its own report on president Johnson. From left to right: John mccloy," j. Lee rankin (general counsel), senator richard russell, congressman gerald ford, chief justice earl warren, president lyndon b. Johnson, allen dulles, senator John sherman cooper, along with congressman hale boggs.

Main informative article: warren commission

Even the president's commission on the assassination of president Kennedy, known publicly as the warren commission, has been set on November 29, 1963, by president Johnson to inquire into the assassination. Its own 888-page ultimate record has been offered to Johnson on september 2-4, 1964, also made people few weeks after. It reasoned that lee harvey Oswald acted independently from the killing of president Kennedy as well as the temptations of Texas governor John connally, also that jack ruby additionally acted independently from the murder of Oswald. [129] the commission's findings and decisions have proven been criticized and encouraged with after research studies.

Even the commission took its unofficial title, "the warren commission", by the chairman," chief justice earl warren. As stated by posted transcripts of all Johnson's presidential mobile discussions, a few significant officials were more in relation to forming this kind of commission, and lots of commission members required part just with extreme hesitation. Some of these primary bookings was a commission could fundamentally make greater controversy than consensus," and also the ones anxieties eventually proved legitimate.

Each of those warren commission's recordings were filed into the national archives at 1964. The unpublished part of the information was sealed for seventy five years (to 2039) underneath an overall countrywide archives plan which put on most national investigations from the executive branch of government, also a span "designed to function as security for innocent individuals who might likewise be broken due to these relationship with members at case". The 75-year rule no longer exists, supplanted from the flexibility of information act of 1966 as well as also the JFK records act of 1992.

Ramsey clark panel

In 1968, a board of 4 professional medical professionals made by attorney general ramsey clark fulfilled in washington, d.c., to test different photos, x-ray pictures, records, along with other signs in regards to the passing of president Kennedy. Even the clark panel ascertained that president Kennedy was struck by two bullets fired from behind him one which manipulates the bottom of their throat onto the most suitable side minus bone and also one opposite which entered the skull from destroyed and behind its top straight side by side the analysis additionally signals the skull taken entered very well over the external occipital protuberance, that had been at odds with all the warren commission's findings.

Rockefeller commission

Even the USA president's commission on cia activities inside the USA was put up under president gerald ford from 1975 to inquire into the actions of their cia over the U.S.. The commission has been directed by vice president nelson rockefeller, also may be called the rockefeller commission.

Section of this commission's function coped with all the Kennedy assassination, namely the mind breeze as noticed from the zapruder movie (very first exhibited into the typical public in 1975), and also the potential existence of e. Howard hunt and frank sturgis at Dallas. The commission reasoned that neither hunt nor sturgis had been in Dallas during time of this assassination.

Church committee

Even the church committee would be the usual term talking about this 1975 united states senate select committee to study governmental operations with respect to intelligence activities, " a U.S. Senate committee chaired by senator frank church, to look into the illegal intelligence gathering from the central intelligence agency (cia) and federal bureau of investigation (fbi) following the watergate episode. Additionally, it researched the cia and FBI behavior about the JFK assassination.

Their report reasoned the analysis around the assassination from FBI and cia had been basically nil and facts which may possibly have heavily influenced the analysis had been offered into the warren commission from those bureaus. The analysis shown there has been a risk that senior officers at the bureaus left aware decisions to not reveal possibly significant info.

United states home select committee on assassinations

Main informative article: united states house select committee on assassinations

Just as a consequence of raising people and statutory doubt about the warren commission's findings and also the transparency of federal government bureaus, residence resolution 1540 has been passed september 1976, producing America house select committee on assassinations (hsca) to inquire into the assassinations of president Kennedy and martin luther king, jr.

Even the committee researched right up until 1978, and also at march 1979 issued its last report, concluding that president John f. Kennedy was probably assassinated as an effect of the conspiracy. The primary grounds behind this decision was, even as stated by the record's dissent, the afterward discredited acoustic investigation from some police station dictabelt recording. The committee reasoned that preceding investigations to Oswald's accountability ended up "detailed and reputable" nevertheless they failed to satisfactorily look into the prospect of the conspiracy, also that federal companies conducted using "various amounts of proficiency". Exclusively, the FBI and cia were also proven to become conducive to sharing advice together with different bureaus and also the warren commission. Rather than supplying all advice related to this analysis, the FBI and cia simply reacted to certain orders and also so were occasionally insufficient. What's more, that the secret service failed to correctly study advice it owned before this assassination and has been prepared to guard the president.

Regarding the decisions of "likely conspiracy", 4 of those a dozen committee members composed dissenting remarks. In compliance with the suggestions of this hsca, the dictabelt acoustic and recording proof another assassin was then reexamined. In light of reports by the fbi's technical services division plus also a especially appointed national academy of sciences committee discovering that "dependable acoustic statistics would not support an end there wasn't a second gunman", " the justice department reasoned "that no persuasive proof might be recognized to further encourage that the idea of the conspiracy at... That the assassination of president Kennedy".

Even though the concluding record also encouraging quantities of this hsca was publicly published, both the working newspapers and chief files have been sealed before 2029 underneath congressional principles and just partially published as a member of their 1992 JFK act.

JFK act along with assassination records review board

Main informative article: president John f. Kennedy assassination records collection act of 1992

In 1992the favorite but controversial picture JFK experienced revived public attention from the assassination and specially from the still-classified records referenced at the picture's post-script. Mainly in reaction to this movie, congress passed the JFK act, " or" president John f. Kennedy assassination records collection act of 1992". The aim of the law was supposed to amass in the national archives and also make publicly offered each the assassination-related data held by national and local agencies, private taxpayers along with several different associations.

Even the JFK act also mandated that the production of a different business office, the assassination records review board, to critique the records that were submitted for both completeness and lasted secrecy. The review board wasn't commissioned to get some findings or decisions about the assassination, simply to get and discharge most of applicable records. By 1994 till 1998, the assassination records review board accumulated and unsealed about 60,000 paperwork, comprising of more than thoUSAnd webpages. Authorities agencies asked some recordings continue being categorized and those were assessed under department criteria for their JFK act. You will find 29,420 this sort of data and everyone them were either partially or fully published, together with strict conditions for redaction.

Even a staff accounts to its assassinations records review board claimed that mind photos from the Kennedy information usually are maybe not of Kennedy's mind and reveal not as much injury than Kennedy continuing. Boswell refuted these allegations. The board also discovered, contradictory together using all the photographic graphics revealing no defect, a range of witnesses, for example in the autopsy and also parkland hospital, watched a big wound from the rear part of the president's thoughts. Even the board and board member, jeremy gunn, have additionally emphasized the troubles with opinion testimony, so requesting visitors to consider most the evidence, together with because of concern because of individual malfunction, and not just take unmarried announcements as "evidence" for a single thought or some other.

Each of staying assassination-related documents (somewhere around 5,000 webpages) have been planned to be published from october 26, 2017, together with the exclusion of records licensed for continuing postponement from the president under these states: (1))"continuing postponement is made mandatory with an identifiable problems for the armed forces, defense, and intelligence operations, and law enforcement, or behavior of international connections" and also (two)"the recognizable injury is of such gravity it outweighs the public interest ." there has been a concern with investigators that large information, especially those of the cia, could still stay categorized following 20 17. Even though these records could consist of exciting historical info, each the information were analyzed with the review board and weren't ascertained to influence the details of this Kennedy assassination. President donald-trump mentioned in oct 20 17 he wouldn't obstruct the discharge of records. About 26 april 2018, the deadline established by president trump to discharge JFK recordings that he halted the launch of several recordings before oct 26, 2021.

Conspiracy theories

Even the wooden fencing in the grassy knoll, at which lots of conspiracy theorists feel still another gunman burst

Main informative article: John f. Kennedy assassination conspiracy theories

Most conspiracy theories purport the assassination included folks or associations along with lee harvey Oswald. Most contemporary concepts help with a legal conspiracy between parties rather varied since the fbi, the cia, " the U.S. Armed forces, " the mafia," vice-president Johnson," Cuban president fidel castro, the kgb, or even any mixture of the things.

Public opinion surveys have always shown a vast majority of all Americans feel there is a conspiracy to get rid of Kennedy. Gallup surveys also have discovered that just 20--30 percent of the populace imagine that Oswald had acted independently. These surveys show there isn't any understanding about who may happen to be included. Previous los angeles district attorney vincent bugliosi believed a number of forty-two bands, eighty-two assassins, along with 2-14 people were detained in many different Kennedy assassination conspiracy theories.

Reactions into the assassination

Even the assassination evoked meaty reactions globally. The very first hour later the shooting has been an occasion of fantastic confusion until the president's departure has been first announced. The episode happened through the cold war, plus it had been initially unsure perhaps the capturing may possibly be a portion of the bigger assault on the U.S. There is concern if vice president Johnson, who'd previously been driving two vehicles behind from the motorcade, had been still safe.

Even the news shocked the state. Individuals cried publicly and assembled from section shops to see the tv policy, even though some others jumped. Targeted visitors in a few regions came to a stop whilst the headlines spread in car to auto. Schools around the USA disregarded their college students first. Anger versus Texas and texans was reported by a few people. A variety of cleveland browns lovers, for instance, carried signals in the following sunday's home match against the Dallas cowboys decrying town of Dallas as "murdered the president".

But there have been instances of Kennedy's opponents cheering the assassination. A journalist documented in the roads of amarillo, using a female yelling outside,"hey, amazing, JFK's croaked!"

Even the event made an enduring impact on a lot of global. Much like the prior assault on pearl harbor of december 7, 1941, and also the next september 11 strikes, requesting "where were you once you learned president Kennedy's assassination" could grow to be an ordinary subject of dialogue.

Artifacts, museums and spots now

Even the airplane that served as air force 1 during that right time of this assassination is really on screen in the national museum of the united states air force in dayton, ohio. The 1961 lincoln continental limo is really on screen in the henry ford museum at dearborn, michigan.

Jacqueline Kennedy's pink lawsuit, " the autopsy file, that the x-rays, along with president Kennedy's blood-stained clothing come from the ownership of this national archives, with entry commanded from the Kennedy family. Different items from the oval include things like gear from parkland hospital injury space; Oswald's gun, journal, along with revolver; bullet items; and also, the windshield of Kennedy's limo. The lincoln catafalque, where president Kennedy's coffin rested at the capitol, is on screen in the united states capitol visitor center.

In 1993 that the three-acre park inside of dealey plaza the structures dealing with this, " the overpass, along with a section of the adjoining railyard -- for example, railway shifting tower -- were all incorporated in the dealey plaza historic district from the national park service. A lot of the location can be found by people, for example, inland and park knoll. Elm avenue continues to be a lively thoroughfare; yet an x painted at the trail marks the approximate place of the pictures struck Kennedy and connally. Even the Texas school book depository and its particular sixth-floor museum attract 325,000 traffic yearly, also comprises are creation of the region that Oswald fired. The sixth floor museum additionally oversees the John fitzgerald Kennedy memorial situated 1 block east of dealey plaza.

In the management of this deceased president's brother, attorney general robert f. Kennedy, several products were ruined from the USA govt. The casket by which president Kennedy's body has been hauled out of Dallas into washington had been dropped to the ocean from the air power, due to the fact "its people display will be exceptionally devastating and in contrast to public policy". Apart from things, the cable label on Oswald's corpse, the catalogue by which Oswald arranged his outfits produced by ruby, and also a window by the Texas school book depository, have been in personal hands-on. The Texas state archives gets got the clothing connally was sporting if he had been taken. The gun ruby was able to destroy Oswald afterwards arrived in to the ownership of ruby's brother earl, also has been marketed in 1991 for about $220,000.

Chapter four

Growing up in the Kennedy family

In all, rose fitzgerald Kennedy will have 9 children, 4 boys and 5 women. She maintained note cards for everyone them at a tiny wooden document and left a place of writing everything down out of a physician's trip into the shoe dimension they'd in a specific era. John fitzgerald Kennedy is appointed in honor of rose's daddy, John francis fitzgerald, also the boston may or popularly called honey fitz. As very long, family members and friends telephoned this tiny psychedelic infant, jack. Jack was a exact healthy newborn, also rose listed on his note-card the youth diseases by which he endured, such like: "whooping cough, measles, chickenpox." on february 20, 19 20 if jack wasn't yet 3 yrs. Of age, " he had been sick of scarlet fever, an extremely infectious after which possibly life-threatening illness. His dad, joseph patrick Kennedy, was fearful little jack could perish. Mr. Kennedy went into the hospital each afternoon to maintain his son's side, also roughly a month after jack chose a twist to the recovered and better. However, jack wasn't incredibly healthful, also as he had been suffering from 1 disease or some other his family was able to joke concerning the large hazard a kitty shot biting him with a number of his bloodstream that the mosquito was nearly positive to expire!

When jack had been, the Kennedys transferred to your brand-new property a couple blocks off in their previous house at brookline, a locality just out boston. It turned out to be a delightful home or apartment with a dozen bedrooms, turreted windows, as well as a large porch. High in energy and vision, jack's dad worked quite difficult in turning into a prosperous business man. After he had been a pupil at harvard higher education and with a tough time fitting as a irish catholic, he declared to himself he'd earn several thoUSAnd dollars from age of 3-5. There has been lots of bias towards irish catholics at boston at the moment, however joseph Kennedy was decided to ensure success. Jack's great-grandparents had originated in ireland and were able to present to their own families, irrespective of lots of insecurities. Jack's grandfathers did better to guys, either becoming dominant boston politicians. Jack, as of most his family needed achieved, can delight in an exact comfortable daily life. The Kennedys had all that they had and much more.

From the full time jack had been there had been seven kids fully. Jack had a elderly brother, joe; 4 sisters, rosemary, kathleen, eunice, along with patricia; and also a young brother, robert. Jean and teddy had not been born but. Nannies and housekeepers aided rose conduct your family.

Joseph p. Kennedy sr. With sons joe jr. Along with jack, palm beach, 1931.

In the very close of the college season, the Kennedy kiddies goes into their summer residence in hyannis port on cape cod at which they appreciated sailing, swimming, and playing touch football. Even the Kennedy kiddies played with hard, plus so they appreciated competing together. Joseph sr. Invited that this particular competition, notably on the list of boys. He had been a dad having rather substantial anticipations and needed the boys to succeed sports and what they strove. Since he said, "if the going gets rough, the tough get started." but these contests proceeded far. 1 time after joe indicated he and jack race in their own bikes, they collided head-on. Joe appeared unscathed whilst jack needed to possess twenty-eight stitches. Due to the fact joe had been just two years old and stronger compared to jack, if they struggled jack would ordinarily buy the worst of this. Jack was not the sole god that introduced some true menace to joe's dominating place while the earliest kid.

Jack was hot and had lots of buddies at choate, a traveling school for teen boys at connecticut. He played with basketball, tennis, soccer, and golf clubs and enjoyed examining. His pal lem billings recalls how strange it was jack needed an everyday subscription for the new york occasions. Jack needed a "smart, individualist mind," his head grasp afterwards noted, nevertheless he wasn't exactly the optimal/optimally university student. He'd not consistently do the job too hard as he would, but history and english, that were his most favorite issues. "today jack," his dad wrote at a letter daily, "i really actually don't wish to provide the belief which i am a nagger, for good knows that i believe that's the worst thing every parent is, and now that i feel you are aware when i did not feel you'd items i'd be charitable within my own attitude on your own failings. Provided that expertise in dividing persons i know you've got items and also you also may really go quite a ways...it's quite hard to create principles you have failed whenever you had been very youthful, and that's the reason why i am advocating one to get exactly the best that you can. I'm not anticipating a great deal, also i am not going to be dissatisfied in case you really don't prove for being always a true genius, however, that i believe that you may be very rewarding citizen together with good decision and comprehension."

Jack graduated from choate and entered harvard in 1936, at which joe was a university student. Just like his brother joe, jack performed with football. He also wasn't nearly as great an athlete like joe however he experienced a great deal of conviction and persistence. Regrettably, one particular afternoon whilst playing with the ruptured a disc in his back. Jack hardly ever recovered in the mishap along with also his spine chose to disturb him to get the remainder of his entire life.

Even the two eldest boys were so captivating, fine, and clever teenage boys and mr. Kennedy had higher hopes to get both of them. But it had been joe who'd announced everyone when he had been a youthful boy which he is the very first catholic to eventually become president. Nobody bothers him for an instant. Jack, on the opposite side, appeared marginally less strenuous. He had been busy in college student classes and athletics plus also he worked in his record and administration courses, even nevertheless his mark stayed just ordinary. Late in 1937," mr. Kennedy was appointed united states ambassador to england and proceeded with his family, with all the exclusion of joe and jack that were in harvard. As a result of his daddy's occupation, jack grew to become incredibly curious in western politics and also world affairs. After having a summer trip to england along with other nations from europe, jack came back into harvard additional excited to know about government and history and also to stay on top of current affairs.

Joe and also jack usually obtained letters out of their dad in england, that advised of the newest news about the battles and worries that everybody else feared could blow into a full-blown warfare. Adolph hitler dominated germany and benito mussolini dominated italy. They had solid arenas and desired to choose property from various other nations. On september 1, 1939, germany invaded poland and world war ii commenced.

From that moment, jack had been a grownup at harvard and made a decision to compose his thesis about why good britain was unprepared for war together with germany. This was published as a publication known why england slept. Back in june 1940, jack graduated from harvard in june. His dad sent him a cablegram from london: "a couple of things that i usually knew about you 1 that you're sensible two that you're a swell man enjoy father."

World war ii plus also a future at politics

So-on after graduating, equally joe and jack joined the navy. Joe was a flyer and also delivered to europe, whilst jack was forced lieutenant (lt.) And delegated south pacific because commander of the patrol torpedo ship, " the pt109.

Rear pp81 lt. (jg) John f. Kennedy, 1942

Lt. Kennedy needed a team of a dozen males whose assignment was supposed to avoid japanese boats out of delivering equipment with their own soldiers. At the evening of august 2, 1943, lt. Kennedy's crew patrolled the seas searching for enemy boats. A western destroyer unexpectedly became observable. Nevertheless, it had been traveling full rate and led right. Maintaining the wheellt. Kennedy attempted to gallop from this manner, however to absolutely no avail. The substantially bigger japanese war-ship rammed the pt 109, dividing it and murdering two of lt. Kennedy's adult men. The rest were able to leap as their ship moved in flames. Lt. Kennedy was banged hard contrary to the cockpit, once-again hammering his feeble spine. Patrick mcmahon, among the team members, experienced dreadful burns up in his hands and face and was prepared to quit up. From the shadow, lt. Kennedy were able to get mcmahon and haul him straight back to where by other lands were relegated to your bit of this ship which has been afloat. At dawn, lt. Kennedy directed his men towards a little island a few miles off. Despite their or her own harms, lt. Kennedy had been competent to tow patrick mcmahon ashore, a strap out of mcmahon's living coat gap between his teeth. Six times after two indigenous islanders located them went to get assistance, bringing an opinion jack experienced thrown in to a slice of coconut shell. A day later, the pt109 team was rescued. Jack's brother joe wasn't lucky. He expired a calendar year after when his airplane hauled up throughout a hazardous assignment in europe.

When he returned residence, jack has been granted the navy and marine corps medal because of his direction and guts. Together with the warfare finally arriving at an end, it had been time for you to pick the type of job he required to really do. Jack had thought learning to be a teacher or perhaps a writer, but together with joe's tragic departure unexpectedly everything shifted. After acute conversations with jack regarding his long run, joseph Kennedy certain that he needs to run for congress at Massachusetts' eleventh rhode island, by which he won 1946. This really was first of jack's governmental profession.

Because the decades moved, John f. Kennedy, a democrat, served a few terms (6 years) at the home of reps, also in 1952 he had been elected for the us senate.

So-on after being chosen senator," John f. Kennedy, in 3-6 decades old, wed 2 4 year-old jacqueline bouvier, a writer using the washington times-herald. Regrettably, early in his marriage, senator Kennedy's straight back began to hurt and he'd two deep surgeries. While coping with operation, " he composed a novel around a few us senators who'd risked their own livelihood to struggle to the matters by that they considered. The publication, named profiles in courage, had been given the pulitzer prize for biography in 1957. The exact identical calendar year, the Kennedys' very first child, caroline, had been created.

John f. Kennedy has turned into a favorite politician. Back in 1956 he had been nearly choosing to operate for president. Kennedy nevertheless determined he would run for president within another election.

He also began functioning long hours and travel around the USA on weekends. On july 13, 1960 the democratic party nominated him as its candidate. Kennedy requested lyndon b. Johnson, a senator in Texas, to conduct together with him vice president. From the election November 8, 1960, Kennedy conquered the republican vice president richard m. Nixon at a exact close race. At age of forty-three, Kennedy was the youngest person elected president and also the very first catholic. Ahead of his inauguration, his next child, John jr., had been created. His dad wanted to telephone him John.

John f. Kennedy gets to be the 35th president of this united states of America

John f. Kennedy was sworn in as the 35th president january 20, 1961. Inside his inaugural address he talked of this demand for most Americans to be more active citizens. "ask not what your country can do to you, ask what you could do to help the own country," he explained. In addition, he questioned the states of this entire world to combine with each other to battle what he termed the "common enemies of man: tyranny, poverty, and illness, and war " president Kennedy, with his spouse and 2 kids, attracted a brand new, young soul towards the whitehouse. Even the Kennedys considered the white house need to be somewhere to celebrate American history, culture, and accomplishment. They encouraged musicians, authors, artists, scientists, musicians, celebrities, and athletes to go to them. Jacqueline Kennedy additionally shared with her spouse's attention in history. Gathering a number of the best furniture and art that the USA had generated, she revived each of the chambers at the white house to create it an area that definitely reflected the USA's historical past and inventive imagination. Everybody else was amazed and enjoyed her work.

Even the white house also looked the same as a enjoyable place for those Kennedys' two young children, caroline and also John John. There has been a preschool a pool, and a treehouse out about the whitehouse yard. President Kennedy was likely the most adorable person inside the nation, however he found the time for you to play and laugh his or her children.

But the president had lots of anxieties. Certainly, one of those matters he feared about was that the chance of atomic war among the USA and the soviet union. He understood when there is a warfare, a large number of individuals will perish. Given that world war ii there had been a great deal of rage and feeling between your 2 states but no firing between American and soviet troops. This 'cold war', that had been unlike some war that the whole world had viewed, " was a truly battle involving the soviet union's greek program of federal government and also the united states' democratic approach. As they distrusted one another, equally states spent large sums of funds assembling weapons. You will find lots of times as soon as the battle between the soviet union and the united states of America might have stopped in atomic warfare, like in Cuba during the 1962 missile disaster or across the town of berlin.

President Kennedy labored hours getting out of bed in 7 and perhaps not planning to sleep before twelve or eleven at night time, or even after. He also read newspapers even though he ate breakfast had encounters together with essential people during your daytime, also read testimonials out of his consultants. He desired to be certain he left the very most effective decisions because of his nation. "i'm asking all one to truly be new leaders at that new frontier,"" he explained. Even the new frontier had not been really a spot but also a style of believing and behaving. President Kennedy desired the USA to proceed forwards in to the near future using brand new discoveries from mathematics and developments in schooling, occupation as well as other areas. He also wanted independence and democracy for the entire environment.

Certainly, one of those very first items president Kennedy did would be to generate the most peace corps. Through the app, that exists now, Americans can volunteer to get the job done any place on the planet at which assistance becomes necessary. They are able to aid in places like farming, education, healthcare, and structure. Lots of young women and men have served as peace corps volunteers also have won the esteem of men and women around the entire world.

President Kennedy was eager for the united states to direct the manner in researching distance. Even the soviet union was prior to the

USA in its own distance application and president Kennedy had been made to grab up. He stated, "no nation that expects to become the pioneer of all different states might get to remain behind within this race for distance " Kennedy has been the president ask congress to accept greater than 22 billion dollars for project apollo, which had the objective of landing an American man to the moon prior to the conclusion of the ten years.

President Kennedy needed to bargain with lots of serious issues here within the U.S. The most significant issue of most was racial discrimination. Even the us supreme court had ruled in 1954 that segregation in public universities wouldn't more be allowed. White and black kiddies, your decision faked, ought to really go to college with them. That was the legislation of this property. But there were various educational institutions, notably in southern countries, that didn't follow that particular law. There has been likewise racial segregation on buses, in restaurants, movie theaters, movie theaters, along with other people spots.

Countless of all Americans united with each other, folks of all backgrounds and races, to protest peacefully this respect.

Martin luther king jr. Was clearly one of many well-known leaders of this movement to civil rights. Most civil rights leaders did not assume president Kennedy was encouraging enough in their own efforts. Even the president considered that carrying people protests would just anger lots of black people today and also make it more difficult to persuade the people of congress who did not accept him to pass on civil rights legislation. From june 1 1, 1963, nevertheless, president Kennedy made a decision that enough time had begun to require more rigorous actions that will help with the civil rights fight. He suggested that the brand-new civil rights bill on the congress, also then he moved television requesting us citizens to finish racism. "100 decades of delay have passed since president lincoln freed the slaves, but their heirs, their grandsons, aren't totally free of charge," he explained. "this country was founded by people of many backgrounds and nations...[and] around the basic principle which most men are made the same " president Kennedy made it crystal clear all Americans, no matter their own skin tone, have to delight in a nice and joyful life at the U.S..

Even the president is shot

But on November 2 1, 1963, president Kennedy flew to Texas to supply a few political speeches. A day later, because his vehicle drove past cheering crowds in Dallas, shots rang out. Kennedy was badly injured and died a short period after. In just a couple of hours of this shooting, the authorities arrested lee harvey Oswald and charged him with the murder. About November 2 4, the other guy, jack ruby, captured and murdered Oswald, so silencing the one individual who would have given more details relating to it dreadful occasion. The warren commission was structured to look into the assassination also to describe the various questions that stayed.

Even the legacy of John f. Kennedy

President Kennedy's departure induced enormous despair and despair among most people in America. Many people remember in which these were what they're doing once they learned that the facts. ThoUSAnds and hundreds of folks assembled in washington for its president's funeral, also countless around the globe observed it about tv.

Just as recent several years have passed and additional presidents have composed their personalities in history," John Kennedy's quick period at office sticks outside from people's reminiscences because of their direction, persona, along with achievements. Most esteem his coolness when up against complicated choices --such as everything to consider soviet missiles from Cuba in 1962. Other individuals respect his own capacity to encourage individuals who have his eloquent speeches. Others assume his empathy as well as also his openness to struggle for brand new administration programs that will help poor people, both the aged and the ailing were important. Just like most leaders, even John Kennedy left mistakes," however, he had been consistently optimistic in regards to the long run. He considered people might fix their ordinary issues should they placed their region's interests and functioned jointly.

Right after noon on November 22, 1963, president John f. Kennedy was assassinated because he rode in a motorcade through dealey plaza in downtown Dallas, Texas.

From the autumn of 1963, president John f. Kennedy along with also his political advisors were still preparing to its upcoming presidential effort. Even though he'd perhaps not officially declared his candidacy, it had been evident that president Kennedy was about to conduct and he looked convinced about his odds to get reelection.

By the conclusion of september, the president went west, talking in two distinct countries in under per weekend. The excursion was intended to place a highlight on organic sources and conservation attempts. However, JFK additionally utilized it to seem outside topics --for example schooling, domestic safety, and also earth peace--because of his conduct at 1964.

Campaigning at Texas

Per month afterwards, the president treated democratic party parties in boston and philadelphia. Afterward, on November 1 2 he even held that the very first major political preparation session to the upcoming election season. In the assembly, JFK emphasized the need for decreasing florida and Texas and spoke to his plans to go to both nations from the following a couple of months.

Mrs. Kennedy would accompany him to the fold during Texas, that are her very first lengthy community appearance as the lack of the newborn, patrick, in august. On November 2 1 the president first woman strangled on air force 1 to its inaugural, five-city excursion of Texas.

President Kennedy was conscious that the feud amongst celebration leaders at Texas could sabotage his opportunities taking their nation in 1964, and also a few of his own intentions for this particular vacation was supposed to attract democrats collectively. In addition, he knew a somewhat smaller but outspoken set of extremists was leading for the governmental anxieties from Texas and could probably make its existence sensed --specially at Dallas, at which us ambassador for the united nations adlai stevenson was attacked per month prior after building a language. None the less, JFK did actually enjoy the possibility of earning washington, becoming from people and in the political fray.

The very first halt was sanatorium. Vice-president lyndon b. Johnson," governor John b. Connally, also senator ralph w. Yarborough headed the composed celebration. They followed the president into brooks air force foundation for its devotion of their aerospace medical health heart. After onto houston, he also addressed that a muslim American taxpayers' company and talked in a testimonial dinner for congressman albert thomas ahead of finishing your afternoon at fort worth.

Early morning in fort value

A mild rain has been decreasing friday afternoon, November 2-2, however, a bunch of a couples of million stood at the parking lot away from the Texas lodge at which in fact the Kennedys had invested the evening time. A stage has been installed and also the president wearing no security from the weather," came outside to produce a short feedback. "you will find really no helpless hubs at fort worth," he commented, "and that i love your being here this afternoon. Mrs. Kennedy is coordinating herself. It requires more, however, clearly, she appears much better than we perform if she's doing it" he moved onto discuss the country's requirement because of staying "next to none" in shield and also at distance, to get continuing growth from the market and "the openness of taxpayers from America to think that the burdens of direction "

The heat of this viewer reaction was so real as the president achieved to shake fingers beneath a sea of grinning faces.

Straight back within the resort the president talked in a breakfast of this fort worth chamber of commerce, emphasizing military planning. "we're nonetheless the keystone in the arch of flexibility," he explained. "we'll carry on to execute...our obligation and those of Texas is likely to be from the guide."

About to Dallas

The presidential party made the resort went from motorcade into carswell air force foundation for its thirteen-minute trip to Dallas. Coming to love field, both president and mrs. Kennedy disembarked and walked into a weapon at which a bunch of well-wishers had accumulated, plus so they spent a few seconds vibration arms.

The very first woman acquired a fragrance of crimson roses, which she attracted her into the awaiting limo. Governor John connally and his wife, nellie, have been seated at the great outdoors up whilst the Kennedys entered and hauled. As it was no more tolerable, the plastic bubble shirt had been abandoned. Vice-president and mrs. Johnson inhabited the other car from the motorcade.

The procession left the airport traveled across a ten-mile path which wound through downtown Dallas along the best way into the trade mart at which in fact the president has been advised to talk in a luncheon.

The assassination

Crowds of enthusiastic individuals lined the roads and waved into the Kennedys. The automobile switched off mainstreet in dealey plaza approximately 12:30 p.m. Because it had been passing that the Texas school book depository, gun fire abruptly reverberated from the plaza.

Bullets struck the president neck and mind along with then he slumped above towards mrs. Kennedy. The sheriff has been taken at his spine.

The automobile sped off to parkland memorial hospital only a few minutes off. But very little can possibly be achieved for its president. A catholic priest had been summoned to manage the very last rites, also in 1:00 p.m. John f. Kennedy was declared dead. Though severely injured, governor connally could regain.

The president's figure has been attracted to enjoy industry and also added to air force 1. Prior to the airplane took a grim-faced lyndon b. Johnson stood at the restricted, crowded compartment and required the oath of office administered by us district court judge sarah hughes. The quick ceremony happened at 2:38 p.m.

Greater than an hour before, authorities had detained lee harvey Oswald, a newly hired worker in the Texas schoolbook depository. He had been held to get its assassination of president Kennedy along with also the deadly shooting, soon subsequently, of patrolman j. D. Tippet to the Dallas road.

On sunday afternoon, November 24," Oswald was planned to be moved from police headquarters into the county prison. Viewers throughout the united states observing the live tv policy suddenly watched a person target a pistol and firing point blank selection. The assailant was known as jack ruby, a neighborhood nightclub proprietor. Oswald died two weeks after at parkland hospital.

The president's funeral

The exact same afternoon, president Kennedy's flag-draped casket was transferred in the white house into the capitol to the caisson drawn by six horses that were grey accompanied by one particular rider less dark horse. In mrs. Kennedy's petition, the cortege along with also other ceremonial particulars were mimicked over the funeral of abraham lincoln. Crowds lined pennsylvania avenue and lots of cried publicly whilst the caisson handed. Throughout the 2-1 hours which the president's body lay in state at the capitol rotunda, roughly 250,000 folks registered by to pay their respects.

On monday, November 25, 1963 president Kennedy had been set to rest in arlington national cemetery. The funeral has been attended by heads of state and agents from at least 100 states, together with countless thoUSAnds and thoUSAnds more watching on tv. Subsequently, in the tomb website, mrs. Kennedy along with also her partner's brothers, robert and edward, lit an eternal fire.

Maybe the funniest pictures of this evening have been that the agree for his dad contributed by very little John f. Kennedy jr. (whose next birthday was), girl caroline kneeling close for her mum in the president bier, along with also the outstanding grace and faith displayed by jacqueline Kennedy.

As individuals across the country and the planet fought to earn sense of the senseless action also to articulate their beliefs of president Kennedy's life and heritage, lots of remembered these phrases out of his own inaugural speech:

This isn't going to be completed at the initial 100 days, nor at the very first 1000 days, nor at the life span with this government. Nor maybe even in our life on the particular planet. But permit us to commence.

Arlington national cemetery

To find out more about president Kennedy's funeral along with tomb website, visit the arlington national cemetery site.

After-math

The warren commission

On November 29, 1963 president lyndon b. Johnson appointed the president's commission on the assassination of president Kennedy. It was called the warren commission following its chairman," earl warren, chief justice of the U.S. President Johnson led the commission to appraise things having to do with the assassination as well as the next killing of the alleged assassin, and also to report its findings and decisions.

Your house select committee on assassinations

Even the united states house of representatives created your home select committee on assassinations from 1976 to re-open the analysis of this assassination in light of allegations that preceding queries had perhaps not got the complete collaboration of national bureaus.

Note for the reader: position 1b from the hyperlink below into this findings of this 1979 house select committee on assassinations says the committee had detected "a higher probability that two gunmen fired" in the president. This decision caused from your lastminute"discovery" of the Dallas police radio broadcast tape which supposedly provided signs that 4 or even four shots have been fired at dealey plaza. Subsequent to the record looked in printing, acoustic pros examined the cassette proved logically that it had been utterly useless --thereby diluting the discovering at stage 1b.

The committee, which likewise researched the passing of dr. Martin luther king jr., issued its record on march 29, 1979.

Assassination documents collection

Throughout the president John f. Kennedy assassination records collection act of 1992, the united states congress ordered that most assassination-related stuff be put with each other under oversight of this national archives and records administration.

Chapter five

The legacy of John f. Kennedy

One of the various monuments into John f. Kennedy, most likely the very notable could be that the sixth floor museum at Dallas, at the construction which has been formerly the Texas school book depository. Annually, almost 350,000 people see where lee harvey Oswald waited November 22, 1963, to take the president's motorcade. The memorial itself is still an oddity for its physical link if it illuminates; yet the memorable--and also eeriest--time of an trip towards the sixth ground would be that if you flip a corner and then deal with the window during which Oswald fired his gun because Kennedy's open up automobile snaked throughout dealey plaza's b-road distances under. The windows have been littered once-again using cardboard boxes, so as they'd been around this bright day when Oswald concealed there.

Traffic from all around the globe have signed up their own titles from the memory novels, and lots of them have composed tributes: "our best president" "oh we miss him" "the best person because jesus christ." as most people come up with the probable conspiracies that caused JFK's assassination. The conflicting truths of Kennedy's lifestyle do not fit his worldwide standing. However, at the opinion of earth, this handsome man turned into a charismatic pioneer that, in his lifetime and also from his passing, functioned as a sign of hope and purpose.

President Kennedy invested than just three years now at the whitehouse. His very first season was a tragedy, since he acknowledged. The bay of pigs invasion of presidential Cuba was the earliest in a run of unsuccessful initiatives to reverse fidel castro's regimen. His first 1961 summit meeting in vienna using all the soviet leader nikita khrushchev has been a embarrassing encounter. The majority of his legislative suggestions expired on capitol hill.

Yet he had been likewise accountable for several outstanding achievements. The absolute most essential, and many renowned, has been that his skillful direction of this Cuban missile crisis in 1962, extensively believed to be one of the most dangerous moment given that world war ii. The majority of his army consultants --they weren't independently --considered the united states of America need to bomb the missile pads which the soviet union had been stationing at Cuba. Kennedy, alert to this chance of escalating the catastrophe, as an alternative purchased a blockade of soviet boats. Sooner or later, a calm agreement had been first reached. Subsequently, each Kennedy and khrushchev started to soften the relationship between washington and moscow.

Kennedy, during his brief presidency, suggested many essential measures ahead. In a speech at American college in 1963, he talked kindly of this soviet union, thus easing the cold war. This afternoon, immediately after two decades of largely averting the matter of civil rights," he presented a language of sophistication that was outstanding, also started a driveway to get a civil rights bill which he expected could stop racial segregation. In addition, he suggested a voting rights administration and national applications to give healthcare for the older and poor people. A few of those suggestions became legislation within his life --a excellent disappointment to Kennedy, that was not very powerful with congress. But the majority of those statements became law right after his passing in part as a result of his successor's political authority, but because they looked the same as a monument into your president.

Kennedy was the youngest person elected into the presidency, achievement the guy that, in the moment, was that the earliest. He represented -- since he realized--a fresh creation and its particular coming of age. He had been the very first president created from the 20th century, also the very first younger veteran of world war ii to accomplish at the whitehouse. John hersey's powerful report of Kennedy's wartime bravery, released from the new yorker at 1944, aided him to establish his political job.

In building his superstar, Kennedy's private charm aided. A witty and articulate speaker that he looked constructed for its period of tv. To see him film now is usually to become struck with the power of his existence and also the humor and beauty of the oratory. His famous inaugural speech was fraught up with phrases which looked built to be forged in rock, as a number have been. Restoring a motto out of his prep school times, even setting your nation instead host to choate, he exhorted us residents: "ask not what your country can do for you--ask what you could do to help your nation "

Still another contributor into the Kennedy legend, even something much more profound compared to his private beauty, would be that the picture of exactly what numerous came into predict elegance. He had elegance, at the feeling of acting and behaving subtly; he had been likewise a person who looked to obtain elegance. He had been handsome and appeared athletic. He had been still wealthy. He'd a captivating spouse and kiddies, a family room. An associate of the journalist ben bradlees, composed a 1964 publication about Kennedy known that distinctive grace.

Even the Kennedys lit-up the white home by authors, artists, and intellectuals: the most renowned cellist pablo casals, the poet robert frost, the french intellectual andré malraux. Kennedy had graduated from harvard, also hauled his government with all the faculty's professors. He gathered his people opinions using quotes from philosophers.

Even the Kennedy family aided make his own livelihood, after, his heritage. He might not reach the presidency with no daddy's assistance. Joseph Kennedy, among the strangest and most callous males in the USA, experienced relied upon his very first kid, joe jr., to input politics. After joe died in the war, his dad's aspirations switched into your next-oldest young child. He paid out to a lot John's--jack's--attempts and also used his own countless attract in fans. He cried to his pal arthur krock, " the new york times, to greatly help jack release his very first publication, why england slept. Years after, when Kennedy wrote profiles in courage together with the assistance of the aide theodore sorensen, k-rock lobbied for its publication to acquire a pulitzer prize.

Even the Kennedy heritage features a darker side too. Before his own presidency, lots of JFK's political coworkers believed him a play boy whose affluent dad experienced bankrolled his attempts. Lots of critics watched recklessness, impatience, impetuosity. Nigel hamilton, the writer of JFK: reckless youth, " a normally admiring analysis of Kennedy's ancient decades, awakened following almost 800 webpages:

He also 'd the wisdom, that the guts, " a self-conscious charm, very good looks, idealism, dollars... Nevertheless, as there, there had been something lost --a definite thickness or severity of motive... After the respondents or even so the ladies were obtained, there clearly was still a definite viciousness on jack's role, a collapse to reverse conquest to whatever very purposeful or deep.

I. F. Stone, the celebrated liberal author, detected in 1973:"he could be an illusion"

Kennedy's picture of childhood and energy will be also, to a level, a dream. He invested his lifetime at hospitals, combating a number of ills. His capacity to function as president has been a bit in isolation.

Far was written regarding Kennedy's secret life. Much like his dad, he had been obsessed with all the ritual of sensual conquest--earlier and throughout his marriage before and throughout his presidency. Whilst he had been living, many ladies, the secret service representatives, and also others that understood of his philandering maintained it that a mystery agent. Even now, today the testimonies of the sexual routines are commonly understood, they've achieved very little to tarnish his standing.

Half a century following his own presidency that the stamina of Kennedy's allure isn't only the consequence of the crafted picture and private allure. Additionally, it displays the historic moment by that he arose. From early 1960s, a lot of the American people had been still willing, even eager, to feel he had been that the guy who'd" get the country going " in some period when all of these united states was prepared to go ahead. Motion and dynamism had been fundamental to Kennedy's allure. Throughout his 1960 presidential effort he maintained sniping in the republicans for 8 decades of stagnation: 'i've premised my effort to get the presidency around the single premise that the American men and women are uncomfortable in the current drift within our federal class... And then they will have the will and also the power to begin the united states of America moving " whilst the historian arthur m. Schlesinger jr.," Kennedy's good friend and advisor, later on composed, "the funding community, somnolent at the eisenhower years' come living... [together with] the discharge of energy that does occur when people who have thoughts have an opportunity to set them in to training "

Kennedy helped provide freedom into this thought of following a more federal intent --a wonderful American assignment. From the 15 decades as world war ii, ideological momentum was steadily growing while in the U.S., fueled by worries concerning the competition with the soviet union and from controversy in regards to the energetic operation of their American market.

When Kennedy won the presidency that the appetite to get shift has been tentative, because his agonizingly lean perimeter more than richard nixon signifies. Nevertheless, it had been climbing, also Kennedy captured as soon as to extend a mission--at least he comprehended that the demand for you --although it wasn't entirely obvious exactly what the assignment was. Early in his tenure, a defense department official composed that a policy paper that voiced a more curious mixture of pressing function and obscure aims:

Even the united states requires a grand goal... We act as when our actual aim is always to sit from our swimming pools contemplating that the tires round our middles... The essential thing isn't that the grand goal be precisely appropriate, it really is that we've got just one and we start off moving.

This mirrored John Kennedy's world view, certainly one of devotion, activity, movements. People that knew him comprehended, but he had been cautious compared to his addresses indicated.

John f. Kennedy proved to be a great president however, maybe not really a great one particular, many scholars agree. A survey of historians at 1982 rated him 13th out from their 3 6 presidents contained from this poll. Thirteen this kind of surveys from 1982 into 2011 set him on average, 12th. Richard neustadt, the most dominant presidential scholar, honored Kennedy throughout his life and has been respected by Kennedy in-turn. Yet at the 1970 she commented: "he will probably soon be only a flicker, permanently obscured from the listing of the successors. I really don't believe history will probably have a lot of distance for John Kennedy."

However, 50 decades following his departure, Kennedy is not even close to "a flicker" he also remains a powerful image of the dropped instant, of the towering idealism and also hopefulness that succeeding generations try to recuperate. His appeal the amorous, nearly mysterious, institutions his title arouses --maybe not merely survives but flourishes. The journalist and historian theodore white, that had been shut to Kennedy, printed a renowned interview for-life magazine together with jackie Kennedy soon following her husband's assassination, where she stated:

In night, until we had got to sleep," jack wanted to engage in a few recordings; and also, the tune he adored all came in the end with this album. The traces he adored to listen were don't allow it to be forgot, that once there is an area, for a single brief shining moment which was called camelot.

Along with so a lyric grew to become the most permanent picture of the presidency.

White, within his memoirs, remembered the reverence Kennedy experienced motivated one of his good friends:

" I still have trouble watching John f. Kennedy crystal clear. The picture of him which comes to me personally... Is really so graceful and clean -- as when i could see him jump the steps up of his air plane for the reason that fifty percent lope, then turn, flinging his arm out at farewell into the audience, just before evaporating inside of. It turned out to be a ballet move.

Friends are maybe not the ones creepy from the Kennedy mystique. He had been learning to be a charismatic figure during his presidency. At the center of 1963, 5 9 per cent of all Americans surveyed promised they had hunted in 1960, but just 49.7 per cent of republicans had really done thus. Right after his departure, his landslide climbed to sixty-five per cent. In gallup's public opinion polls," he always has the maximum approval rating of any president since franklin d. Roosevelt.

Even the situation of Kennedy's death turned into a nationwide obsession. A large number of novels are released concerning his assassination," the majority of these rejecting the warren commission's conclusion that lee harvey Oswald acted independently. Subsequent to the assassination, actually robert f. Kennedy, the president's brother spent --perhaps times --calling visitors to consult whether there'd been a conspiracy, even before he comprehended his queries can hurt their or her own livelihood. For the particular day, roughly 60 per cent of all Americans genuinely believe that Kennedy dropped prey to some conspiracy.

"there was an epic refuge to John f. Kennedy's government that'd nothing more to do using all the mists of camelot,"" david talbot, the creator of salon, composed many decades back. His publication screenplay: the hidden history of the Kennedy years, even more intense compared to many Kennedy conspiracy theories, also implied the president daring, innovative intentions --and also the threats he introduced to entrenched passions --prompted a plot to shoot his own lifetime span.

There really are several factors to issue the state variant of Kennedy's murder. However, there's not much concrete evidence to establish any one of those concepts --which the mafia, the fbi, the cia, or even perhaps lyndon b. Johnson has been included. A few folks state that his passing was a consequence of washington's covert initiatives to destroy castro. For several Americans, it stretches credulity to simply accept an event therefore epochal may be clarified while the action of a still-mysterious loner.

Well until the people began jerking on conspiracy theories, Kennedy's murder attained immense proportions. Inside his 1965 novel, a lot of days," schlesinger utilized words effusive they appear to be unctuous now, nevertheless during exactly the period that they weren't considered surplus or mawkish: "it had been gone today," he composed of their assassination: "the life-affirming, life-enhancing zest, the genius, the humor, that the trendy devotion, the purpose"

Just like all of presidents, Kennedy experienced failures and successes. His government had been ruled with a notable variety of issues and disasters --from berlin, Cuba, laos, and viet nam; in georgia, mississippi, and alabama. One of them, " he handled adroitly and, even on occasion, courageously. A lot of he could barely fix. He had been a booked, sane guy who never shown fire.

Yet lots of people watched him and do as an idealistic and, yes, even fervent president who'd have shifted the country and also the entire world, had lived. His heritage has just increased at the fifty years since his passing. He embodies a rare moment of people activism points out a lot of the ongoing allure: he also reminds a lot of Americans of the era as it managed to trust that politics can talk into society ethical yearnings and also be exploited into its own highest ambitions. Greater than that, possibly, Kennedy reminds us at a moment after the world's skills appeared endless when its own prospective looked unbounded, when Americans felt they might clear up hard issues and achieve daring deeds.